The Cold War's Turning Points: Kennedy's Decisions

Copyright Page

TITLE: The Cold War's Turning Points: Kennedy's Decisions

1ST Edition

Copyright @ 2023

ISBN: 9798223983071

Table of Contents

The Cold War's Turning Points: Kennedy's Decisions

By Roberto Miguel Rodriguez

Chapter 1: Kennedy's Diluted Bay of Pigs Invasion Created One Year Later the Cuban Missile Crisis

The Origins of the Bay of Pigs Invasion

In the annals of the Cold War, few events have had as profound an impact on the course of history as the Bay of Pigs invasion. This ill-fated military operation, orchestrated by the United States under President John F. Kennedy's administration, was a critical turning point that ultimately led to the Cuban Missile Crisis.

The origins of the Bay of Pigs invasion can be traced back to the escalating tensions between the United States and the Soviet Union during the Cold War. Fidel Castro's rise to power in Cuba in 1959, which resulted in the establishment of a communist regime just miles off the coast of Florida, greatly alarmed the American government. The fear of a Soviet-backed communist state so close to its borders fueled the desire to remove Castro from power.

Kennedy's decision to proceed with a diluted version of the invasion plan in April 1961 was influenced by various factors, including Cold War politics. The new president was eager to prove his toughness against communism, and the Bay of Pigs invasion seemed like an opportunity to do so. Additionally, Kennedy faced pressure from influential anti-Castro Cuban exiles in the United States who hoped to reclaim their homeland.

However, the invasion quickly turned into a disaster. The Cuban military, with support from the Soviet Union, swiftly defeated the ill-prepared and poorly executed operation. The failure of the Bay of Pigs invasion not only embarrassed the United States but also emboldened Castro's regime and strengthened its ties with the Soviet Union.

The public perception of Kennedy's handling of the Bay of Pigs invasion and the subsequent Cuban Missile Crisis was mixed. While some praised his ability to defuse the missile crisis without resorting to war, others criticized his initial decision to authorize the invasion and subsequent miscalculations. The media played a significant role in shaping public opinion during these events, with both positive and negative coverage influencing public perception.

The significance of the Bay of Pigs invasion and the Cuban Missile Crisis cannot be overstated in terms of shaping the global balance of power during the Cold War. The failed invasion highlighted the limitations of American military intervention and signaled to the Soviet Union that the United States was vulnerable to defeat. This perception ultimately emboldened the Soviet Union to deploy nuclear missiles to Cuba, precipitating the Cuban Missile Crisis and bringing the world closer to nuclear war than ever before.

In conclusion, the origins of the Bay of Pigs invasion can be traced back to the Cold War politics and the fear of Soviet-backed communism in America's backyard. Kennedy's decision-making during this critical period was influenced by these factors, as well as the public perception and media coverage surrounding the events. The failure of the invasion and the subsequent Cuban Missile Crisis had far-reaching implications, shaping the global balance of power and highlighting the dangerous brinkmanship of the Cold War era.

The Eisenhower Administration's Plan for Overthrowing Castro

In the midst of the Cold War, the Eisenhower administration developed a covert plan to overthrow Fidel Castro's regime in Cuba. This plan, known as Operation Pluto, laid the groundwork for future

U.S. involvement in Cuban affairs and had far-reaching implications for the global balance of power during this critical period.

Operation Pluto was conceived in response to concerns about the spread of communism in the Western Hemisphere, particularly in Cuba. The Eisenhower administration believed that Castro's rise to power posed a significant threat to U.S. interests, as his government aligned itself with the Soviet Union and implemented socialist policies.

The plan involved training and arming Cuban exiles who would then launch a military invasion of Cuba with the goal of overthrowing Castro's regime. The Central Intelligence Agency (CIA) was heavily involved in the planning and execution of the operation, working closely with anti-Castro groups in Cuba.

However, the Eisenhower administration's plan was not fully implemented before President John F. Kennedy took office in January 1961. Kennedy inherited Operation Pluto and faced a crucial decision regarding its execution. He ultimately chose to proceed with a modified version of the plan, which became known as the Bay of Pigs invasion.

Kennedy's decision to proceed with the diluted invasion had significant consequences. The invasion, which took place in April 1961, was a resounding failure. The Cuban military quickly crushed the invading forces, leading to embarrassment for the United States and a strengthening of Castro's regime. This failure had a lasting impact on Kennedy's presidency, as it highlighted the dangers of U.S. intervention in foreign affairs and shaped his approach to future crises, including the Cuban Missile Crisis.

The public perception of Kennedy's handling of the Bay of Pigs invasion and the Cuban Missile Crisis was heavily influenced by the media. The media played a critical role in shaping public opinion, with many newspapers and television networks criticizing Kennedy's handling of both crises. This public perception further impacted Kennedy's decision-making and added pressure to resolve the Cuban Missile Crisis diplomatically.

Overall, the Eisenhower administration's plan for overthrowing Castro set the stage for future U.S. involvement in Cuban affairs and had a lasting impact on the global balance of power during the Cold War. The failure of the Bay of Pigs invasion and the subsequent Cuban Missile Crisis highlighted the dangers of U.S. intervention and shaped Kennedy's decision-making during this critical period. Historians continue to study these events to understand the complexities of Cold War politics and their long-term consequences.

Kennedy's Inherited Responsibility: Evaluating the Situation

Introduction:

The events surrounding the Bay of Pigs invasion and the Cuban Missile Crisis are widely regarded as two critical turning points in the Cold War. President John F. Kennedy faced immense challenges and inherited a complex situation that required careful evaluation. This subchapter will delve into the crucial aspects that historians need to consider when analyzing Kennedy's decisions during these crises. It will explore the diluted Bay of Pigs invasion and its role in shaping the later Cuban Missile Crisis, the influence of Cold War politics on Kennedy's decision-making, the public perception of his handling of these crises, the media's impact on shaping public opinion, and the significance of these events in shaping the global balance of power during the Cold War.

1. Kennedy's Diluted Bay of Pigs Invasion Created One Year Later the Cuban Missile Crisis:

Kennedy inherited the Bay of Pigs invasion plan from the Eisenhower administration. However, he made critical modifications that ultimately led to its failure. By evaluating the consequences of this unsuccessful operation, historians can understand how it laid the groundwork for the subsequent Cuban Missile Crisis and the heightened tensions between the United States and the Soviet Union.

2. The Role of Cold War Politics in Shaping Kennedy's Decision-Making:

Cold War politics significantly influenced Kennedy's decisions during these crises. Historians must assess the pressure he faced to demonstrate American strength and commitment to combating communism while avoiding nuclear conflict. Understanding these political dynamics is crucial in comprehending the options available to Kennedy and the constraints he faced.

3. The Public Perception of Kennedy's Handling of the Bay of Pigs Invasion and the Cuban Missile Crisis:

Historians must analyze how the public perceived Kennedy's handling of these crises. Kennedy's public image as a young, charismatic leader shaped the way people viewed his decisions. Evaluating public opinion provides insight into the pressures he faced and the impact of his decisions on domestic and international support.

4. The Role of the Media in Shaping Public Opinion:

The media played a significant role in shaping public opinion during the Bay of Pigs invasion and the Cuban Missile Crisis. Historians must examine the media's portrayal of these events, including the dissemination of information, the impact of news coverage on public sentiment, and the potential bias that may have influenced public perception.

5. The Significance of the Bay of Pigs Invasion and the Cuban Missile Crisis in Shaping the Global Balance of Power:

These two events had far-reaching implications for the global balance of power during the Cold War. Historians should explore how the Bay of Pigs invasion and the Cuban Missile Crisis affected superpower relations, the arms race, and the overall stability of the world order. This analysis will shed light on the lasting impact of these crises on the course of the Cold War.

Conclusion:

Understanding Kennedy's inherited responsibility during the Bay of Pigs invasion and the Cuban Missile Crisis requires a comprehensive evaluation of various factors. By examining the diluted invasion plan, the influence of Cold War politics, public perception, media's role, and the global significance of these events, historians can gain valuable insights into the decision-making process and the profound impact of these crises on the Cold War era.

The Decision to Proceed with a Covert Invasion

Title: The Decision to Proceed with a Covert Invasion: A Turning Point in the Cold War

Introduction:

The decision to proceed with a covert invasion is a pivotal moment in the Cold War, as it marked the beginning of a series of events that would forever alter the global balance of power. This subchapter delves into the intricacies of Kennedy's decision-making during the Bay of Pigs invasion and the Cuban Missile Crisis, shedding light on the role of Cold War politics, public perception, media influence, and the lasting impact on the global stage.

Kennedy's Diluted Bay of Pigs Invasion Created One Year Later the Cuban Missile Crisis:

The failed Bay of Pigs invasion, initiated in April 1961, had significant implications for Kennedy's decision-making during the Cuban Missile Crisis in October 1962. The diluted nature of the Bay of Pigs operation, influenced by Cold War politics and strategic considerations, left Castro's regime intact and emboldened the Soviet Union in its support for Cuba. As a result, Kennedy faced increased pressure to take decisive action, leading to the subsequent Cuban Missile Crisis.

The Role of Cold War Politics in Shaping Kennedy's Decision-Making:

Cold War politics played a vital role in shaping Kennedy's decision-making process during both the Bay of Pigs invasion and the Cuban Missile Crisis. The fear of communism's spread, the desire to maintain America's global leadership, and the delicate balance of power between the United States and the Soviet Union heavily influenced Kennedy's choices. The subchapter explores how these factors shaped his approach to covert operations and the subsequent escalation of tensions.

The Public Perception of Kennedy's Handling:

The public perception of Kennedy's handling of the Bay of Pigs invasion and the Cuban Missile Crisis varied significantly. While some praised his leadership in defusing the missile crisis, others criticized his initial mishandling of the Bay of Pigs invasion. This subchapter analyzes the public's perception of Kennedy's decision-making, highlighting the impact on his presidency and the broader Cold War narrative.

The Role of Media in Shaping Public Opinion:

The media played a crucial role in shaping public opinion during both the Bay of Pigs invasion and the Cuban Missile Crisis. Journalistic coverage of these events, from the failed invasion to the tense standoff, influenced public sentiment and impacted Kennedy's decision-making. This subchapter delves into the media's influence and its implications for the broader understanding of these turning points in history.

The Significance of the Bay of Pigs Invasion and the Cuban Missile Crisis:

Both the Bay of Pigs invasion and the Cuban Missile Crisis hold immense significance in shaping the global balance of power during the Cold War. The failed invasion revealed flaws in American covert operations, and the subsequent missile crisis highlighted the dangers of nuclear brinkmanship. This subchapter explores the lasting impact of these events on the Cold War narrative, the Soviet-American relations, and the subsequent arms race.

Conclusion:

The decision to proceed with a covert invasion marked a turning point in the Cold War, leading to one of the most critical moments in history. Kennedy's decision-making during the Bay of Pigs invasion and the Cuban Missile Crisis was shaped by Cold War politics, public perception, media influence, and the significant impact on the global balance of power. Understanding the complexities of these events is crucial for historians and enthusiasts alike as we continue to analyze and learn from these transformative moments in history.

The Execution and Failure of the Bay of Pigs Invasion

The Bay of Pigs invasion stands as one of the pivotal moments in the Cold War era, shaping not only the immediate political landscape but also the global balance of power. Addressing historians who specialize in this period, this subchapter delves into the intricacies of Kennedy's decisions during the Bay of Pigs invasion and the subsequent Cuban Missile Crisis, highlighting the significance of these events in shaping Cold War politics.

One year after the Bay of Pigs invasion, the world witnessed the Cuban Missile Crisis, a direct consequence of Kennedy's diluted approach to the initial invasion. By failing to provide sufficient air support and withholding critical information from the invasion force, Kennedy inadvertently pushed the Soviet Union to install nuclear missiles in Cuba, sparking the most dangerous confrontation of the Cold War. This subchapter delves into the link between the two events, emphasizing how the failure of the Bay of Pigs invasion set the stage for the Cuban Missile Crisis.

Kennedy's decision-making process during these events was heavily influenced by Cold War politics. Fearing a direct confrontation with the Soviet Union and keen to maintain a delicate balance, Kennedy's choices were often shaped by the larger geopolitical considerations of the time. This subchapter explores the intricate web of Cold War politics that influenced Kennedy's actions, shedding light on the complex factors at play.

Public perception of Kennedy's handling of the Bay of Pigs invasion and the Cuban Missile Crisis played a significant role in shaping the narrative surrounding these events. This subchapter examines how Kennedy's initial popularity took a hit in the aftermath of the failed invasion, and how his handling of the Cuban Missile Crisis helped to restore public confidence in his leadership. It delves into the complexities of public opinion and its impact on the political landscape.

The role of the media in shaping public opinion during these events cannot be overstated. This subchapter dissects the media's coverage of the Bay of Pigs invasion and the Cuban Missile Crisis, highlighting its influence on public sentiment, political discourse, and decision-making. It explores the power of media narratives in shaping historical events and shaping public perception.

Ultimately, the significance of the Bay of Pigs invasion and the Cuban Missile Crisis extends far beyond their immediate consequences. This subchapter illuminates how these events shifted the global balance of power during the Cold War, profoundly impacting the dynamics between the United States, the Soviet Union, and the rest of the world. It analyzes the long-term implications of these events and their lasting effects on the international stage.

In conclusion, this subchapter caters to historians, providing a comprehensive analysis of the execution and failure of the Bay of Pigs invasion. It explores the interconnectedness of these events with the Cuban Missile Crisis, Cold War politics, public perception, media influence, and the global balance of power. By delving into these aspects, it offers valuable insights into the complexities of this crucial period in history.

The Invasion Plan and Its Flaws

In the annals of the Cold War, few events have had as far-reaching consequences as the Bay of Pigs invasion and the Cuban Missile Crisis. These two pivotal moments in history, both directly linked to President John F. Kennedy's decision-making, not only shaped the global balance of power during the Cold War but also had a profound impact on the public perception of his leadership.

Kennedy's diluted Bay of Pigs invasion, which took place in April 1961, was a defining moment in the superpower struggle between the United States and the Soviet Union. The invasion plan, devised by the Central Intelligence Agency (CIA), sought to overthrow the Cuban revolutionary government led by Fidel Castro. However, the flawed plan suffered from a lack of sufficient air support and a failure to secure the element of surprise. These critical flaws ultimately led to the invasion's failure and left Kennedy grappling with the consequences.

One year later, in October 1962, the world teetered on the brink of nuclear war during the Cuban Missile Crisis. The crisis was a direct result of the Soviet Union's decision to deploy nuclear missiles in Cuba, within striking distance of the United States. Cold War politics played a significant role in shaping Kennedy's decision-making during this tense standoff. Faced with the potential for an all-out nuclear conflict, Kennedy pursued a strategy of brinkmanship, seeking a diplomatic solution while maintaining a strong military posture.

The public perception of Kennedy's handling of both the Bay of Pigs invasion and the Cuban Missile Crisis was deeply influenced by the media. The media played a crucial role in shaping public opinion, highlighting the flaws in the invasion plan and exposing the dangers of the missile crisis. The intense scrutiny and criticism that Kennedy faced from the media had a lasting impact on his presidency.

These events also had a profound impact on the global balance of power during the Cold War. The Bay of Pigs invasion and the Cuban Missile Crisis heightened tensions between the United States and the Soviet Union and brought the world closer to nuclear war than ever before. These events underscored the dangers of the superpower rivalry and prompted a renewed focus on arms control and détente.

In conclusion, the flawed invasion plan of the Bay of Pigs and the subsequent Cuban Missile Crisis are pivotal turning points in the Cold War. Kennedy's decision-making during these events, influenced by Cold War politics and shaped by media coverage, had a lasting impact on his presidency and the global balance of power. The lessons learned from these events continue to resonate, reminding us of the dangers of miscalculation and the importance of diplomatic solutions in times of crisis.

The Role of CIA and Military Advisors in the Operation

In the dramatic events of the Bay of Pigs invasion and the Cuban Missile Crisis, the role of the CIA and military advisors was significant and highly influential. This subchapter will delve into the crucial involvement of these actors, shedding light on their impact on decision-making, public perception, and the global balance of power during the Cold War.

During the Bay of Pigs invasion, President John F. Kennedy heavily relied on the expertise and advice of the CIA and military advisors. With the aim of overthrowing Fidel Castro's communist regime, the CIA meticulously planned and executed the operation. However, due to a series of miscalculations and faulty intelligence, the invasion ended in a disastrous failure. This failure had far-reaching consequences, as it not only weakened the credibility of the United States but also emboldened Castro and his alliance with the Soviet Union.

The Cuban Missile Crisis, one year later, presented a grave threat to American national security. The CIA played a crucial role in gathering intelligence on the Soviet Union's installation of nuclear missiles in Cuba. This intelligence was vital in shaping Kennedy's decision-making process, as it provided evidence of the Soviet Union's aggressive intentions. The military advisors, working closely with the CIA, formulated military strategies and options for Kennedy to consider. Their expertise and analysis guided the President in his response to the crisis, ultimately leading to the successful resolution of the conflict and the removal of the missiles from Cuba.

The public perception of Kennedy's handling of the Bay of Pigs invasion and the Cuban Missile Crisis was greatly influenced by the role of the CIA and military advisors. The failure of the Bay of Pigs invasion was seen as a major setback for the United States, leading to widespread criticism of Kennedy's leadership. However, the successful resolution of the Cuban Missile Crisis redeemed Kennedy's image, as he was perceived to have made the right decisions in the face of a nuclear threat.

The media played a crucial role in shaping public opinion during these crises. The CIA and military advisors worked closely with the media to control the narrative and shape public perception. Through carefully crafted press releases and briefings, they sought to present a united front and justify their actions to the American people.

Overall, the role of the CIA and military advisors in the Bay of Pigs invasion and the Cuban Missile Crisis cannot be underestimated. Their involvement shaped Kennedy's decisions, influenced public opinion, and had a significant impact on the global balance of power during the Cold War. Understanding their role is crucial for historians seeking to analyze and comprehend these turning points in the Cold War era.

The Unexpected Resistance from Cuban Forces

In the annals of history, few events have had such far-reaching consequences as the Bay of Pigs invasion and the Cuban Missile Crisis. These two pivotal moments during the Cold War not only shaped the global balance of power but also revealed the complexities of decision-making and the role of public perception in international affairs. At the heart of these events was President John F. Kennedy, whose diluted Bay of Pigs invasion inadvertently set the stage for the Cuban Missile Crisis a year later.

Kennedy's decision to proceed with the Bay of Pigs invasion was influenced by the intricate web of Cold War politics. The United States, driven by fears of communism and the spread of Soviet influence in the Western Hemisphere, sought to overthrow Fidel Castro's regime in Cuba. However, the plan was fraught with internal disagreements, lack of coordination, and faulty intelligence, which ultimately led to unexpected resistance from Cuban forces.

Cuban forces, fiercely loyal to Castro, proved to be a formidable opponent for the ill-prepared CIA-trained exiles. The invasion, initially intended to spark a popular uprising against Castro, instead encountered fierce resistance and was swiftly crushed. The unexpected resilience of Cuban forces caught the United States off guard and exposed the flaws in their intelligence-gathering and operational planning.

The public perception of Kennedy's handling of the Bay of Pigs invasion was a critical turning point. The failed operation was seen as a major blunder, tarnishing the image of the Kennedy administration and undermining confidence in their ability to effectively confront the Soviet threat. The media played a crucial role in shaping public opinion, highlighting the failures of the invasion and casting doubt on the administration's decision-making process.

The significance of the Bay of Pigs invasion and the subsequent Cuban Missile Crisis cannot be overstated. These events not only revealed the high stakes and inherent risks of Cold War politics but also pushed the world to the brink of nuclear war. The failed invasion served as a wake-up call for the United States, prompting a reassessment of their approach to Cuba and ultimately leading to the discovery of Soviet missile installations on the island.

In conclusion, the unexpected resistance from Cuban forces during the Bay of Pigs invasion played a pivotal role in shaping the course of history. Kennedy's diluted invasion inadvertently set the stage for the Cuban Missile Crisis, highlighting the complexities of decision-making in the face of Cold War politics. The public perception of Kennedy's handling of these events, shaped by the media, further influenced the global balance of power and the perception of the United States as a superpower. These turning points continue to be studied and analyzed by historians, shedding light on the intricacies of the Cold War and the role of individuals in shaping world events.

The International Response and Lack of Support

In examining the turning points of the Cold War, one cannot overlook the international response and the lack of support that President Kennedy faced during the Bay of Pigs invasion and the Cuban Missile Crisis. These two pivotal moments in history were not only shaped by Kennedy's decisions but also by the complex web of Cold War politics and the global balance of power.

Kennedy's diluted Bay of Pigs invasion, which took place in April 1961, was an attempt to overthrow the communist regime of Fidel Castro in Cuba. However, the operation was poorly planned and executed, leading to its ultimate failure. The international response to this invasion was one of surprise and disappointment. Kennedy had hoped for support from other countries, particularly those in Latin America, but he found little backing. This lack of international support not only weakened the operation but also damaged Kennedy's credibility on the global stage.

One year later, the Cuban Missile Crisis unfolded, bringing the world to the brink of nuclear war. Kennedy's decision-making during this crisis was heavily influenced by the Cold War politics of the time. The crisis erupted when the United States discovered that the Soviet Union was secretly deploying nuclear missiles in Cuba, just 90 miles off the coast of Florida. Kennedy's response was a delicate balance of diplomacy and military brinkmanship, as he sought to avoid a nuclear confrontation while also defending American interests.

The public perception of Kennedy's handling of both the Bay of Pigs invasion and the Cuban Missile Crisis was mixed. The failure of the Bay of Pigs invasion was seen as a significant setback for Kennedy, who had promised to take a tough stance against communism. The Cuban Missile Crisis, on the other hand, was seen as a testament to Kennedy's leadership and ability to navigate a dangerous situation.

The role of the media in shaping public opinion during these events cannot be overstated. The media's coverage of the Bay of Pigs invasion was critical, exposing the botched operation and further damaging Kennedy's reputation. During the Cuban Missile Crisis, the media played a crucial role in informing the public about the gravity of the situation and the potential consequences of a nuclear war.

Both the Bay of Pigs invasion and the Cuban Missile Crisis had far-reaching implications for the global balance of power during the Cold War. The failure of the Bay of Pigs invasion allowed Castro's regime to solidify its power in Cuba and establish a closer alliance with the Soviet Union. The Cuban Missile Crisis, on the other hand, demonstrated the potential for nuclear war and led to a reevaluation of Cold War policies by both the United States and the Soviet Union.

In conclusion, the international response and lack of support that President Kennedy faced during the Bay of Pigs invasion and the Cuban Missile Crisis were significant factors in shaping these turning points of the Cold War. The events not only highlighted the role of Cold War politics in Kennedy's decision-making but also underscored the importance of public perception and media influence. Moreover, the consequences of these events reverberated throughout the global balance of power, leaving a lasting impact on the course of the Cold War.

The Aftermath and Lessons Learned

In the annals of Cold War history, few events have had as profound an impact as the Bay of Pigs invasion and the Cuban Missile Crisis. These two critical turning points not only tested President John F. Kennedy's resolve and decision-making skills but also had far-reaching consequences for global politics. As historians reflect on these events, they uncover valuable lessons that shed light on the complexities of the Cold War era.

Kennedy's Diluted Bay of Pigs Invasion Created One Year Later the Cuban Missile Crisis

One cannot discuss the aftermath of the Bay of Pigs invasion without acknowledging its direct link to the Cuban Missile Crisis. Kennedy's decision to proceed with a scaled-back invasion in 1961, rather than the full-scale assault initially planned by the CIA, had unintended consequences. It not only failed to overthrow the Castro regime but also emboldened Soviet Premier Nikita Khrushchev to deploy nuclear missiles to Cuba as a deterrent against future American interventions.

The role of Cold War politics in shaping Kennedy's decision-making during the Bay of Pigs invasion and the Cuban Missile Crisis

Cold War politics played a pivotal role in shaping Kennedy's decisions during these crises. Faced with the threat of communism spreading to the Western Hemisphere, Kennedy felt compelled to take action. However, the fear of triggering a nuclear war and the need to maintain American credibility in the eyes of its allies added complexity to his decision-making process.

The public perception of Kennedy's handling of the Bay of Pigs invasion and the Cuban Missile Crisis

Public perception of Kennedy's handling of these crises varied significantly. While some admired his resolve and commitment to defending American interests, others criticized his perceived missteps and lack of transparency. The Bay of Pigs invasion was seen as a failure, tarnishing Kennedy's image, but his handling of the Cuban Missile Crisis, particularly his diplomatic approach, earned him praise.

The role of the media in shaping public opinion during the Bay of Pigs invasion and the Cuban Missile Crisis

The media played a crucial role in shaping public opinion during these events. The coverage of the Bay of Pigs invasion exposed the flaws in the operation, leading to public disillusionment. Conversely, the media's reporting during the Cuban Missile Crisis heightened tensions and created a sense of urgency among the American public, increasing their support for Kennedy's actions.

The significance of the Bay of Pigs invasion and the Cuban Missile Crisis in shaping the global balance of power during the Cold War

Both the Bay of Pigs invasion and the Cuban Missile Crisis had a profound impact on the global balance of power during the Cold War. The failed invasion exposed the limitations of American covert operations and emboldened the Soviet Union. The Cuban Missile Crisis, on the other hand, marked a critical turning point, as the world stood on the brink of nuclear war. It led to a reevaluation of the superpowers' strategies and a realization of the need for diplomatic solutions to avoid catastrophic consequences.

In conclusion, the aftermath of the Bay of Pigs invasion and the Cuban Missile Crisis offers valuable lessons for historians and sheds light on the intricate dynamics of the Cold War era. These events highlight the interplay between politics, public opinion, and media influence, while also shaping the global balance of power. Understanding Kennedy's decisions and their consequences is essential to comprehending the complexities of this pivotal period in history.

Political Fallout for Kennedy and His Administration

The Bay of Pigs invasion in April 1961 and the Cuban Missile Crisis in October 1962 were two of the most critical events during the Cold War era. These events not only tested President John F. Kennedy's leadership abilities but also had far-reaching political consequences for him and his administration.

Kennedy's diluted Bay of Pigs invasion, which aimed to overthrow Fidel Castro's regime in Cuba, was a disaster that ended in failure. The invasion was poorly planned and executed, resulting in the capture and humiliation of the US-backed Cuban exiles. The failure of the operation exposed Kennedy's lack of experience and raised questions about his ability to handle the complexities of Cold War politics.

However, it was the Bay of Pigs invasion that set the stage for the subsequent Cuban Missile Crisis. The failed invasion made Castro more determined to seek Soviet assistance, leading to the installation of Soviet nuclear missiles in Cuba. This development brought the United States and the Soviet Union to the brink of nuclear war. Kennedy's decisions during the Cuban Missile Crisis were crucial in defusing the situation and avoiding a catastrophic conflict.

The public perception of Kennedy's handling of both the Bay of Pigs invasion and the Cuban Missile Crisis was mixed. While some admired his resolve and ability to navigate through a dangerous crisis, others criticized his initial missteps and lack of transparency. Kennedy's approval ratings fluctuated during this period, reflecting the divided opinions of the American public.

The media played a significant role in shaping public opinion during these events. Journalists closely covered the Bay of Pigs invasion and the Cuban Missile Crisis, providing constant updates and analysis. The media's reporting influenced public sentiment and contributed to the perception of Kennedy's leadership. The intense media scrutiny also forced Kennedy to be cautious and calculated in his decision-making.

The significance of the Bay of Pigs invasion and the Cuban Missile Crisis in shaping the global balance of power during the Cold War cannot be overstated. These events highlighted the dangers of brinkmanship and the potential consequences of a nuclear conflict. The Cuban Missile Crisis, in particular, led to a reevaluation of US-Soviet relations and the establishment of direct communication channels between the two superpowers to prevent future crises.

In conclusion, the political fallout for Kennedy and his administration following the Bay of Pigs invasion and the Cuban Missile Crisis was multifaceted. These events exposed Kennedy's vulnerabilities as a leader but also demonstrated his ability to navigate through dangerous crises. The public perception of Kennedy's handling of these events was mixed, and the media played a significant role in shaping public opinion. Ultimately, the significance of these events in shaping the global balance of power during the Cold War cannot be understated.

Analyzing the Intelligence Failures

The intelligence failures that occurred during the Bay of Pigs invasion and the Cuban Missile Crisis were pivotal moments in the Cold War. These events not only shaped the global balance of power but also had a profound impact on President John F. Kennedy's decision-making and the public perception of his leadership.

The Bay of Pigs invasion, which took place in April 1961, was a failed attempt by the United States to overthrow the communist regime of Fidel Castro in Cuba. One of the key intelligence failures was the failure to accurately assess the strength of Castro's military forces. The CIA had believed that the invasion would spark a popular uprising against Castro, but this assumption proved to be incorrect. As a result, the invading force was quickly overwhelmed, leading to a humiliating defeat for the United States.

This intelligence failure had far-reaching consequences. It not only undermined Kennedy's credibility and damaged his reputation, but it also created a sense of vulnerability within the United States. The failed invasion made it clear to the Soviet Union that the United States was willing to take aggressive actions in its backyard, which ultimately led to the Cuban Missile Crisis the following year.

The Cuban Missile Crisis, which occurred in October 1962, was the closest the world came to nuclear war during the Cold War. The crisis was sparked when the United States discovered that the Soviet Union was secretly installing nuclear missiles in Cuba. This revelation shocked the American public and raised fears of a potential nuclear attack on U.S. soil.

One of the key intelligence failures during the Cuban Missile Crisis was the failure to detect the Soviet missile buildup in Cuba earlier. This failure meant that the United States was caught off guard and had to scramble to develop a response. It also highlighted the shortcomings of U.S. intelligence agencies in gathering accurate and timely information.

The intelligence failures of the Bay of Pigs invasion and the Cuban Missile Crisis had a profound impact on the global balance of power. The United States' failure in the Bay of Pigs invasion emboldened the Soviet Union and led to increased Soviet support for Cuba. This support, in turn, set the stage for the installation of nuclear missiles in Cuba during the Cuban Missile Crisis. The crisis itself brought the world to the brink of nuclear war and highlighted the dangerous escalation of the Cold War.

In conclusion, the intelligence failures of the Bay of Pigs invasion and the Cuban Missile Crisis were significant turning points in the Cold War. These failures not only shaped President Kennedy's decision-making but also had a profound impact on the public perception of his leadership. Furthermore, these events played a crucial role in shaping the global balance of power during the Cold War. The failures underscored the importance of accurate and timely intelligence in navigating the complexities of the Cold War and avoiding catastrophic consequences.

Revisiting the Decision-Making Process

In the riveting subchapter "Revisiting the Decision-Making Process" of the book "The Cold War's Turning Points: Kennedy's Decisions in the Bay of Pigs and Cuban Missile Crisis," historians and enthusiasts of Cold War history are invited to delve deep into the intricate web of events surrounding these two crucial moments in American history. This subchapter aims to shed new light on the decisions made by President John F. Kennedy and explore their far-reaching consequences that shaped the global balance of power during the Cold War.

One of the central themes explored in this subchapter is the connection between Kennedy's diluted Bay of Pigs invasion and the subsequent Cuban Missile Crisis. Through meticulous research and analysis, the author elucidates how the failed invasion inadvertently led to the Soviet Union's decision to deploy nuclear missiles in Cuba. By revisiting the decision-making process, historians gain valuable insights into the role of Cold War politics in shaping Kennedy's choices during these critical episodes.

Moreover, this subchapter delves into the public perception of Kennedy's handling of the Bay of Pigs invasion and the Cuban Missile Crisis. By examining contemporaneous accounts and public opinion polls, the author uncovers a nuanced understanding of how these events were perceived by the American people. By exploring the role of the media in shaping public opinion, historians gain a comprehensive understanding of the influence exerted by the press during this period.

Notably, this subchapter also highlights the profound significance of the Bay of Pigs invasion and the Cuban Missile Crisis in shaping the global balance of power during the Cold War. By analyzing the political and military ramifications, historians can grasp the magnitude of these events in altering the trajectory of the Cold War conflict. The author underscores the enduring impact of these episodes, which reverberated far beyond the boundaries of the United States and the Soviet Union.

In conclusion, "Revisiting the Decision-Making Process" offers historians a captivating exploration of the Bay of Pigs invasion and the Cuban Missile Crisis, shedding new light on Kennedy's decision-making and their profound consequences. By examining the interplay between Cold War politics, public perception, media influence, and global power dynamics, this subchapter provides a comprehensive and thought-provoking analysis of these pivotal moments in history.

The Impact on Cold War Dynamics and Relations with Cuba

"The Impact on Cold War Dynamics and Relations with Cuba"

The Cold War era was a time of intense global tension and rivalry between the United States and the Soviet Union, with Cuba emerging as a pivotal player in this geopolitical struggle. This subchapter explores the profound impact of two critical events, the Bay of Pigs invasion and the Cuban Missile Crisis, on Cold War dynamics and relations with Cuba.

The Kennedy administration's diluted Bay of Pigs invasion in April 1961 played a significant role in shaping subsequent events. Intended as a covert operation to overthrow Fidel Castro's communist regime, it ended in failure and embarrassment for the United States. This botched attempt not only weakened Kennedy's credibility but also intensified Cold War politics. The invasion's aftermath fueled Castro's determination to solidify his alliance with the Soviet Union, ultimately leading to the Cuban Missile Crisis.

The Cuban Missile Crisis of October 1962 was a direct consequence of the Bay of Pigs invasion. The discovery of Soviet nuclear missiles in Cuba sparked a tense standoff between the superpowers, bringing the world to the brink of nuclear war. Kennedy's handling of the crisis showcased his deftness in navigating the delicate balance between aggression and diplomacy. His decision to impose a naval blockade and negotiate a peaceful resolution with the Soviets averted catastrophe, but also marked a turning point in Cold War dynamics.

Public perception of Kennedy's handling of both the Bay of Pigs invasion and the Cuban Missile Crisis was deeply influenced by Cold War politics. While the invasion was initially met with public support and portrayed as a noble endeavor, its failure led to widespread criticism of Kennedy's decision-making. In contrast, his handling of the Cuban Missile Crisis was largely lauded as a triumph of leadership, bolstering his image both domestically and internationally.

The role of the media in shaping public opinion during these events cannot be understated. The Bay of Pigs invasion and the Cuban Missile Crisis were extensively covered by the press, with media portrayals influencing public sentiment. The media's scrutiny of Kennedy's actions during these crises further highlighted the significance of Cold War politics in shaping decision-making and public perception.

In conclusion, the Bay of Pigs invasion and the Cuban Missile Crisis had far-reaching implications for Cold War dynamics and relations with Cuba. These events not only contributed to the escalation of tensions between the superpowers but also highlighted the critical role of Cold War politics in shaping Kennedy's decision-making. Furthermore, the public perception of these crises, influenced by media coverage, and their impact on the global balance of power during the

Cold War cannot be overstated. By examining these turning points, historians can gain valuable insights into the complex dynamics of this turbulent era.

Chapter 2: The Role of Cold War Politics in Shaping Kennedy's Decision-Making during the Bay of Pigs Invasion and the Cuban Missile Crisis

The Cold War Context

The Cold War, a period of intense political and military tension between the United States and the Soviet Union, served as the backdrop for two pivotal events in American history: the Bay of Pigs invasion and the Cuban Missile Crisis. These events, both occurring during John F. Kennedy's presidency, were shaped by the complex web of Cold War politics and had significant implications for the global balance of power.

Kennedy's Diluted Bay of Pigs Invasion Created One Year Later the Cuban Missile Crisis

The Bay of Pigs invasion, launched by the CIA with the intention of overthrowing Fidel Castro's communist regime in Cuba, ended in a disastrous failure. The invasion, planned under the previous Eisenhower administration, was approved by Kennedy but significantly scaled back. Kennedy's decision to reduce US air support and withhold promised naval support ultimately undermined the mission's chances of success. This failed operation had far-reaching consequences, as it not only solidified Castro's hold on power but also emboldened the Soviet Union to strengthen its alliance with Cuba.

The Role of Cold War Politics in Shaping Kennedy's Decision-Making

Cold War politics played a central role in shaping Kennedy's decision-making during both the Bay of Pigs invasion and the Cuban Missile Crisis. The United States was deeply invested in containing the spread of communism, and Cuba was seen as a strategic ally of the Soviet Union. Kennedy's decisions were influenced by the fear of communist expansion and the desire to maintain American credibility in the face of Soviet aggression. The intense rivalry between the superpowers and the ideological struggle between capitalism and communism heavily influenced Kennedy's approach to these crises.

The Public Perception of Kennedy's Handling of the Crises

Public perception of Kennedy's handling of the Bay of Pigs invasion and the Cuban Missile Crisis was mixed. The failure of the Bay of Pigs invasion initially led to criticism of Kennedy's leadership and decision-making. However, his handling of the Cuban Missile Crisis, in which he successfully negotiated the removal of Soviet missiles from Cuba, earned him widespread praise. The perception of Kennedy as a strong and decisive leader grew in the aftermath of this crisis, bolstering his public image.

The Role of the Media in Shaping Public Opinion

The media played a crucial role in shaping public opinion during both the Bay of Pigs invasion and the Cuban Missile Crisis. The media coverage of the Bay of Pigs invasion highlighted the failure of the operation and contributed to the negative perception of Kennedy's leadership. During the Cuban Missile Crisis, however, the media's portrayal of Kennedy as a resolute leader who stood up to Soviet aggression helped to rally public support for his actions. The media's influence on public opinion during these events demonstrated the power it held in shaping the narrative surrounding the Cold War.

The Significance of the Crises in Shaping the Global Balance of Power

Both the Bay of Pigs invasion and the Cuban Missile Crisis had significant implications for the global balance of power during the Cold War. The failure of the Bay of Pigs invasion solidified Cuba's alliance with the Soviet Union, increasing Soviet influence in the Western Hemisphere. The Cuban Missile Crisis, on the other hand, demonstrated the danger of nuclear brinkmanship and the potential for catastrophic consequences. This crisis led to a period of détente between the United States and the Soviet Union, as both sides recognized the need to avoid direct confrontation. The events surrounding these crises highlighted the precarious nature of the Cold War and the potential for global conflict.

The US-Soviet Rivalry and Nuclear Arms Race

The US-Soviet rivalry and the subsequent nuclear arms race were pivotal aspects of the Cold War era. This subchapter delves into the interconnected nature of these events and their profound impact on global politics during the Kennedy administration. Historians studying this period will find valuable insights into the intertwined events of the Bay of Pigs invasion and the Cuban Missile Crisis, as well as their implications for the balance of power during the Cold War.

Kennedy's diluted Bay of Pigs invasion, which took place in April 1961, inadvertently set the stage for the Cuban Missile Crisis a year later. The failed invasion had far-reaching consequences, as it exposed the United States' covert attempts to overthrow Fidel Castro's regime. This humiliation fueled Castro's desire for protection from the United States, leading him to seek Soviet assistance, ultimately resulting in the installation of nuclear missiles on Cuban soil.

Cold War politics played a significant role in shaping Kennedy's decision-making during both the Bay of Pigs invasion and the Cuban Missile Crisis. The fear of communist expansion and the desire to maintain the credibility of the United States as the leader of the free world heavily influenced Kennedy's actions. The subchapter explores the intricate dynamics of these political pressures and their impact on Kennedy's choices.

Public perception of Kennedy's handling of these crises was deeply divided. While some praised his resolve during the Cuban Missile Crisis, others criticized his perceived weakness during the Bay of Pigs invasion. The subchapter investigates the factors that shaped public opinion, including the role of the media in shaping the narrative. The media's portrayal of these events significantly influenced public sentiment, contributing to the divergent views of Kennedy's leadership.

The significance of both the Bay of Pigs invasion and the Cuban Missile Crisis in shaping the global balance of power cannot be overstated. These events heightened tensions between the United States and the Soviet Union, bringing the world to the brink of nuclear war. The subchapter explores how these crises led to a reevaluation of nuclear strategy, arms control negotiations, and the establishment of a hotline communication system between the two superpowers.

In conclusion, the US-Soviet rivalry and the nuclear arms race were integral to the Cold War, and the events of the Bay of Pigs invasion and the Cuban Missile Crisis were significant turning points. Historians studying Kennedy's decisions and the subsequent impact on global politics will find valuable insights in this subchapter, shedding light on the complex dynamics of the era and the lasting consequences of these events.

The Rise of Fidel Castro and Cuban-Soviet Relations

In the subchapter "The Rise of Fidel Castro and Cuban-Soviet Relations," we delve into the complex interplay between Fidel Castro's ascent to power and the subsequent deepening of Cuban-Soviet relations. This pivotal period in history set the stage for the events that unfolded during the Bay of Pigs invasion and the Cuban Missile Crisis, both of which had profound implications for the global balance of power during the Cold War.

To understand the rise of Fidel Castro, one must first examine the socio-political climate of Cuba in the 1950s. The corrupt regime of Fulgencio Batista had created a fertile ground for a revolutionary movement, and Castro emerged as a charismatic leader who promised to bring social justice and equality to the Cuban people. Through a combination of guerrilla warfare, political maneuvering, and popular support, Castro successfully overthrew Batista's regime in 1959, establishing a socialist government.

Castro's rise to power and his subsequent alignment with the Soviet Union was met with mixed reactions. For some, particularly those in the United States, Castro's socialist policies and close ties with the Soviet Union were seen as a threat to American interests in the region. This perception was further fueled by the nationalization of American-owned businesses in Cuba and Castro's land reforms, which targeted wealthy Cuban landowners, many of whom had close ties to the United States.

The Cuban-Soviet alliance, while beneficial for Castro's government, also served the strategic interests of the Soviet Union. By establishing a presence in Cuba, the Soviets gained a foothold in the Western Hemisphere, posing a direct challenge to American hegemony in the region. Castro, in turn, relied on Soviet economic and military aid to strengthen his hold on power and defend against potential American aggression.

The significance of this alliance became evident during the Bay of Pigs invasion in 1961. Kennedy's decision to support a covert operation aimed at overthrowing Castro's government proved to be a disastrous miscalculation. The invasion, although initially conceived as a decisive blow against Castro, was poorly executed and lacked adequate support. The failure of the Bay of Pigs invasion not only embarrassed the United

States but also solidified Castro's grip on power and pushed him further into the arms of the Soviet Union.

The Cuban Missile Crisis, which unfolded a year later, was the culmination of these events. The discovery of Soviet missile installations in Cuba brought the world to the brink of nuclear war. Kennedy's handling of the crisis, characterized by a combination of diplomatic negotiations and a show of military strength, has been the subject of much debate and analysis. The public perception of Kennedy's handling of both the Bay of Pigs invasion and the Cuban Missile Crisis was mixed, with some praising his leadership and others criticizing his initial missteps.

The role of the media during these events cannot be overstated. Journalists played a crucial role in shaping public opinion and influencing the narrative surrounding these crises. Their reporting, often biased and sensationalized, further polarized public opinion and fueled the already intense Cold War tensions.

In conclusion, the rise of Fidel Castro and the deepening of Cuban-Soviet relations during the Cold War played a pivotal role in shaping Kennedy's decision-making during the Bay of Pigs invasion and the Cuban Missile Crisis. The significance of these events in shaping the global balance of power cannot be overstated, as they brought the world to the brink of nuclear war and forever altered the dynamics of the Cold War. A thorough understanding of these turning points is essential for historians seeking to comprehend the intricacies of Kennedy's decision-making process, the role of Cold War politics, the public perception of these events, and the media's impact on shaping the narrative.

The Strategic Importance of Cuba

Cuba, a small island nation located just 90 miles off the coast of Florida, played a pivotal role in the Cold War and became a strategic battleground for the United States and the Soviet Union. The subchapter "The Strategic Importance of Cuba" delves into the geopolitical significance of this Caribbean nation, its impact on the global balance of power during the Cold War, and the events that unfolded under Kennedy's presidency.

Throughout the Cold War, Cuba served as a key player in the ideological struggle between the United States and the Soviet Union. Its proximity to the United States made it a potential launching pad for Soviet missiles, posing a direct threat to American national security. Moreover, Cuba's alliance with the Soviet Union allowed the Soviets to establish a strategic foothold in the Western Hemisphere, challenging American hegemony in the region.

Kennedy's diluted Bay of Pigs invasion in 1961 had far-reaching consequences that would shape Cuba's role in the Cold War. The failed invasion not only exposed the United States' covert operations but also solidified Fidel Castro's grip on power, leading to his alignment with the Soviet Union. This, in turn, set the stage for the Cuban Missile Crisis in 1962, when the Soviet Union attempted to install nuclear missiles in Cuba. The crisis brought the world to the brink of nuclear conflict and tested Kennedy's leadership in managing the escalating tensions.

The public perception of Kennedy's handling of the Bay of Pigs invasion and the Cuban Missile Crisis was a crucial aspect that shaped his decision-making. The subchapter explores how Kennedy's ability to navigate the complex political landscape of the Cold War was not only influenced by the strategic importance of Cuba but also by the need to maintain public support and confidence in his presidency. The media played a significant role in shaping public opinion during these events, and Kennedy had to carefully manage the narrative to ensure his decisions were perceived favorably.

Looking at the broader context, the Bay of Pigs invasion and the Cuban Missile Crisis had a profound impact on the global balance of power during the Cold War. These events heightened tensions between the United States and the Soviet Union, leading to increased arms races, nuclear proliferation, and the establishment of a hotline between the two superpowers to prevent future misunderstandings. Cuba became a symbol of the ideological struggle between communism and democracy, and its strategic importance continued to shape global politics for years to come.

In conclusion, the subchapter "The Strategic Importance of Cuba" highlights the crucial role of Cuba in the Cold War and its significance in shaping Kennedy's decision-making during the Bay of Pigs invasion and the Cuban Missile Crisis. It explores the interplay between Cold War politics, public perception, media influence, and the global balance of power, providing historians with a comprehensive understanding of these turning points in the Cold War era.

Kennedy's Cold War Policy and Its Implications

Kennedy's Cold War policy had far-reaching implications that shaped the global balance of power during this critical period in history. This subchapter delves into the key turning points in Kennedy's decisions during the Bay of Pigs invasion and the Cuban Missile Crisis, exploring the role of Cold War politics, public perception, and the media.

One year after the diluted Bay of Pigs invasion, the world witnessed the Cuban Missile Crisis, a direct consequence of Kennedy's initial handling of the failed invasion. The subchapter examines how Kennedy's decision to withhold air support and limit the scope of the invasion in 1961 inadvertently emboldened Soviet leader Nikita

Khrushchev to deploy nuclear missiles in Cuba, sparking the most intense standoff of the Cold War. By tracing the connections between these events, historians gain valuable insights into the intricate web of Cold War politics and their implications for Kennedy's decision-making.

Furthermore, this subchapter explores the public perception of Kennedy's handling of the Bay of Pigs invasion and the Cuban Missile Crisis. It delves into the stark contrast between the initial public support for Kennedy during the Bay of Pigs invasion and the subsequent disillusionment following the Cuban Missile Crisis. By analyzing the impact of these events on Kennedy's popularity, historians gain a deeper understanding of the challenges faced by leaders during times of crisis and the enduring consequences of their decisions.

In addition to public perception, the subchapter investigates the role of the media in shaping public opinion during these pivotal moments of the Cold War. It explores how the media's coverage of the Bay of Pigs invasion and the Cuban Missile Crisis influenced public sentiment, highlighting the power of media narratives in shaping historical events. By examining the dynamics between the media and political decision-making, historians can better comprehend the complexities of Cold War politics and the role of information dissemination in shaping global events.

Ultimately, this subchapter emphasizes the significance of the Bay of Pigs invasion and the Cuban Missile Crisis in shaping the global balance of power during the Cold War. By unpacking the complex interplay between political decisions, public perception, and media influence, historians gain a comprehensive understanding of the lasting implications of these events. Through this analysis, the subchapter aims to contribute to a nuanced understanding of Kennedy's Cold War policy and its profound impact on the course of history.

Kennedy's Approach to Containing Communism

In the subchapter titled "Kennedy's Approach to Containing Communism," we delve into the pivotal role that President John F. Kennedy played in addressing the spread of communism during the Cold War. This subchapter explores the connection between Kennedy's decisions in the Bay of Pigs invasion and the Cuban Missile Crisis, shedding light on how these events shaped the global balance of power and influenced Kennedy's decision-making process.

The first section of this subchapter focuses on the correlation between Kennedy's diluted Bay of Pigs invasion and the subsequent Cuban Missile Crisis. Historians have long debated the cause-and-effect relationship between these two events, analyzing how the failure of the Bay of Pigs invasion may have contributed to the Soviet Union's decision to deploy nuclear missiles in Cuba. By examining Kennedy's decisions and actions during these critical moments, we gain insight into his approach to containing communism.

Next, we delve into the role of Cold War politics in shaping Kennedy's decision-making during the Bay of Pigs invasion and the Cuban Missile Crisis. The complex geopolitical landscape of the Cold War heavily influenced Kennedy's choices, as he sought to balance the containment of communism with avoiding a nuclear conflict. Understanding the intricate web of alliances, rivalries, and ideological tensions during this time is crucial to comprehending Kennedy's approach to these crises.

The public perception of Kennedy's handling of the Bay of Pigs invasion and the Cuban Missile Crisis is explored in the subsequent section. We analyze how the media portrayed Kennedy's decisions, the impact of the crisis on his popularity, and his efforts to manage the public's perception of the events. This section provides a unique perspective on the intersection of politics, public opinion, and historical memory.

Furthermore, we examine the role of the media in shaping public opinion during the Bay of Pigs invasion and the Cuban Missile Crisis. The media played a significant role in disseminating information and shaping public understanding of these events. Understanding the media's influence during this period is vital in comprehending the broader implications of Kennedy's decisions.

Finally, we discuss the significance of the Bay of Pigs invasion and the Cuban Missile Crisis in shaping the global balance of power during the Cold War. These events had far-reaching consequences, not only in terms of superpower relations but also in redefining the strategies and tactics employed during the Cold War. Exploring the lasting impact of these crises provides historians with valuable insights into this pivotal era in world history.

Overall, this subchapter serves to illuminate Kennedy's approach to containing communism, drawing on the specific context of the Bay of Pigs invasion and the Cuban Missile Crisis. By analyzing the interplay between historical events, political decision-making, public perception, media influence, and global power dynamics, historians gain a deeper understanding of the Cold War's turning points and their lasting effects.

Balancing Domestic and International Considerations

In the annals of Cold War history, few events stand out as prominently as Kennedy's decisions in the Bay of Pigs invasion and the Cuban Missile Crisis. These two critical moments not only defined his presidency but also had a profound impact on the global balance of power during the Cold War era. In this subchapter, we delve into the intricate interplay between domestic and international considerations that influenced Kennedy's decision-making during these pivotal moments.

Kennedy's Diluted Bay of Pigs Invasion Created One Year Later the Cuban Missile Crisis

One cannot fully comprehend the Cuban Missile Crisis without understanding the Bay of Pigs invasion that preceded it. Kennedy's decision to support a covert operation against Fidel Castro's regime, led by Cuban exiles, proved disastrous. The invasion, which had initially aimed to overthrow Castro, resulted in failure and embarrassment for the United States. This setback played a crucial role in shaping Kennedy's subsequent approach to the Cuban Missile Crisis, as he sought to rectify the mistakes made during the Bay of Pigs.

The Role of Cold War Politics in Shaping Kennedy's Decision-Making

The Cold War politics of the time heavily influenced Kennedy's decision-making process during both the Bay of Pigs invasion and the Cuban Missile Crisis. The intense rivalry between the United States and the Soviet Union, along with the fear of communist expansion, colored Kennedy's strategic calculations. Balancing the need to protect American national security interests while avoiding a direct military confrontation with the Soviet Union posed a formidable challenge for the young president.

The Public Perception of Kennedy's Handling

Public perception of Kennedy's handling of these crises played a significant role in shaping his decision-making. The Bay of Pigs invasion was seen as a failure, leading to a loss of credibility for Kennedy's administration. However, his resolute stance during the Cuban Missile Crisis, which ultimately resulted in the removal of Soviet missiles from Cuba, boosted public confidence in his leadership.

Kennedy's ability to rally the nation and project strength in the face of a potential nuclear standoff solidified his reputation as a steadfast leader.

The Role of Media in Shaping Public Opinion

The media played a crucial role in shaping public opinion during the Bay of Pigs invasion and the Cuban Missile Crisis. The extensive coverage of these events brought the realities of the Cold War to the American living room, heightening the sense of fear and urgency. The media's portrayal of Kennedy's response to the crises influenced public sentiment, further highlighting the delicate balance between domestic politics and international considerations.

The Significance of These Crises in Shaping the Global Balance of Power

Both the Bay of Pigs invasion and the Cuban Missile Crisis had far-reaching implications for the global balance of power during the Cold War. These events highlighted the dangers of brinkmanship and the potential for nuclear catastrophe. The resolution of the Cuban Missile Crisis, through diplomacy rather than military conflict, set a precedent for future negotiations between the superpowers. It also underscored the importance of strategic restraint and cooperation in managing global crises.

In this subchapter, we have explored the intricate relationship between domestic and international considerations that shaped Kennedy's decision-making during the Bay of Pigs invasion and the Cuban Missile Crisis. These events not only impacted Kennedy's presidency but also had a profound effect on the global balance of power during the Cold War era. By understanding the complexities of these crises, historians gain valuable insights into the challenges faced by leaders during times of intense geopolitical tension.

The Pressure to Act decisively against Castro

In the midst of the Cold War, President John F. Kennedy faced immense pressure to act decisively against Fidel Castro and his communist regime in Cuba. This subchapter delves into the various factors that contributed to this pressure and analyzes their impact on Kennedy's decision-making during two crucial moments of the era: the Bay of Pigs invasion and the Cuban Missile Crisis.

Cold War politics played a pivotal role in shaping Kennedy's approach to these events. The United States was locked in a global struggle against the spread of communism, and Cuba, situated just 90 miles off the coast of Florida, became a significant hotspot. The fear of a communist stronghold in the Western Hemisphere was a cause for alarm, and Kennedy felt compelled to act in order to maintain the balance of power.

The public perception of Kennedy's handling of the Bay of Pigs invasion and the Cuban Missile Crisis further fueled the pressure on the President. The failed Bay of Pigs invasion in 1961 was seen as a major setback for the United States, and Kennedy's reputation suffered as a result. He was determined not to appear weak in the face of communist aggression, which added to the pressure he faced to take decisive action during the Cuban Missile Crisis in 1962.

The media played a significant role in shaping public opinion during these events. The coverage of the Bay of Pigs invasion highlighted the shortcomings of the operation and intensified the pressure on Kennedy to respond forcefully. The media's portrayal of the President's handling of the Cuban Missile Crisis was crucial in shaping public support for his decisions. Kennedy understood the power of public opinion and recognized the need to maintain a strong image in the eyes of the American people.

The significance of the Bay of Pigs invasion and the Cuban Missile Crisis in shaping the global balance of power during the Cold War cannot be overstated. These events served as turning points, exposing the vulnerabilities of both the United States and the Soviet Union. Kennedy's diluted Bay of Pigs invasion in 1961 inadvertently paved the way for the Cuban Missile Crisis one year later, which brought the world to the brink of nuclear war. The repercussions of these events reverberated throughout the Cold War, solidifying the United States' determination to contain communism and shaping the global dynamics of the era.

In conclusion, the pressure to act decisively against Castro was a driving force in Kennedy's decision-making during the Bay of Pigs invasion and the Cuban Missile Crisis. Cold War politics, public perception, media influence, and the global balance of power all contributed to the intensity of this pressure. Understanding the complexities of these factors provides crucial insight into the events that shaped the Cold War and Kennedy's legacy.

The Impact of Cold War Politics on Decision-Making

The Cold War's Turning Points: Kennedy's Decisions in the Bay of Pigs and Cuban Missile Crisis

Introduction:

In the annals of history, few events have had as far-reaching consequences as the Bay of Pigs invasion and the Cuban Missile Crisis. These two pivotal moments during the Cold War era not only shaped the global balance of power but also had a profound impact on decision-making within the Kennedy administration. This subchapter explores the intricate relationship between Cold War politics and President Kennedy's decision-making process during these critical events.

Kennedy's Diluted Bay of Pigs Invasion Created One Year Later the Cuban Missile Crisis:

One cannot fully comprehend the significance of the Cuban Missile Crisis without understanding its connection to the Bay of Pigs invasion. Kennedy's decision to proceed with a limited invasion of Cuba in 1961 not only failed to remove Fidel Castro from power but also inadvertently set the stage for the subsequent crisis. The invasion's failure exposed the weakness of U.S. covert operations and emboldened the Soviet Union to enhance its presence in Cuba, leading to the installation of nuclear missiles on the island the following year.

The Role of Cold War Politics in Shaping Kennedy's Decision-Making:

Cold War politics heavily influenced Kennedy's decision-making process during both the Bay of Pigs invasion and the Cuban Missile Crisis. The prevailing fear of communist expansion, coupled with the pressure to contain Soviet influence, compelled Kennedy to take decisive action. The need to maintain the credibility of the United States as a superpower and uphold the principles of the Monroe Doctrine played a crucial role in shaping his decisions.

The Public Perception of Kennedy's Handling of the Bay of Pigs Invasion and the Cuban Missile Crisis:

Public opinion played a crucial role in how Kennedy approached these events. While the Bay of Pigs invasion was widely seen as a failure, Kennedy's handling of the Cuban Missile Crisis was viewed as a resolute and successful response to the Soviet threat. The contrasting public perceptions of these two events influenced Kennedy's decision-making, as he sought to redeem himself after the Bay of Pigs debacle.

The Role of the Media in Shaping Public Opinion:

The media's role in shaping public opinion during the Bay of Pigs invasion and the Cuban Missile Crisis cannot be overstated. The media's coverage of these events influenced public sentiment and put pressure on Kennedy to take decisive action. The power of images and narratives disseminated through various media outlets played a significant role in shaping the public's perception of the events and ultimately impacted Kennedy's decision-making process.

The Significance of the Bay of Pigs Invasion and the Cuban Missile Crisis in Shaping the Global Balance of Power:

Both the Bay of Pigs invasion and the Cuban Missile Crisis had far-reaching consequences in shaping the global balance of power during the Cold War. The failed invasion highlighted the limitations of U.S. covert operations and diminished American credibility, while the Cuban Missile Crisis brought the world perilously close to nuclear war. These events served as critical turning points that reshaped the dynamics of the Cold War and underscored the need for diplomacy and strategic decision-making in an era defined by the threat of nuclear annihilation.

Conclusion:

The impact of Cold War politics on decision-making during the Bay of Pigs invasion and the Cuban Missile Crisis cannot be understated. Kennedy's response to these events was shaped by the fear of communist expansion, the pressure to maintain U.S. credibility, and the influence of public opinion. The significance of these events extends beyond their immediate consequences, as they reshaped the global balance of power and underscored the need for careful decision-making in a nuclear-armed world. Understanding the intricate relationship between Cold War politics and decision-making is crucial for historians seeking to unravel the complexities of this era.

The Fear of Soviet Expansion and Domino Theory

The fear of Soviet expansion and the domino theory were influential factors in shaping the decisions of President John F. Kennedy during the Bay of Pigs invasion and the Cuban Missile Crisis. These events, occurring just one year apart, showcased the high stakes and intense Cold War politics that dominated the era.

Kennedy's diluted Bay of Pigs invasion, which took place in April 1961, demonstrated the United States' fear of Soviet expansion in the Western Hemisphere. The invasion was initially planned as a full-scale military operation to overthrow Fidel Castro's communist regime in Cuba. However, due to concerns about provoking Soviet retaliation or a broader conflict, Kennedy decided to reduce the scale of the invasion, resulting in its failure. This decision was influenced by the domino theory, a prevailing belief at the time that if one country fell to communism, neighboring countries would soon follow suit. The fear was that Cuba, under Soviet influence, would become a launching pad for spreading communism throughout Latin America.

The Cuban Missile Crisis, which occurred in October 1962, further intensified fears of Soviet expansion. The discovery of Soviet nuclear missiles in Cuba, capable of striking major US cities, raised the specter of a direct confrontation between the two superpowers. Kennedy's decision-making during this crisis was heavily influenced by the desire to prevent the spread of communism and maintain the global balance of power. He engaged in a tense standoff with Soviet Premier Nikita Khrushchev, ultimately leading to a negotiated settlement that removed the missiles from Cuba.

The public perception of Kennedy's handling of these events was mixed. While some praised his firm stance during the Cuban Missile Crisis, others criticized the failure of the Bay of Pigs invasion. The media played a significant role in shaping public opinion, with newspapers and television broadcasts providing constant coverage of these events. The media's portrayal of Kennedy's decisions and their consequences influenced how the public perceived his leadership during the Cold War.

In the broader context, both the Bay of Pigs invasion and the Cuban Missile Crisis had profound implications for the global balance of power. The failed invasion highlighted the limitations of US military intervention and exposed the vulnerability of the United States in its efforts to contain Soviet influence. The Cuban Missile Crisis, on the other hand, demonstrated the potential for catastrophic nuclear war and the need for diplomatic solutions to prevent further escalation.

In conclusion, the fear of Soviet expansion and the domino theory played a significant role in shaping Kennedy's decisions during the Bay of Pigs invasion and the Cuban Missile Crisis. These events, and their subsequent impact on public perception, the media, and the global balance of power, are crucial turning points in the Cold War narrative. Understanding the historical context and the complex motivations behind these decisions is essential for historians studying this pivotal period in international relations.

The Influence of Hawks and Doves within the Administration

One of the most critical aspects in understanding President Kennedy's decision-making during the Bay of Pigs invasion and the Cuban Missile Crisis is the influence of hawks and doves within his administration. This subchapter aims to shed light on the different perspectives and policy preferences held by these two factions, and how they shaped key decisions made during these turning points of the Cold War.

The hawks, characterized by their aggressive and confrontational stance towards the Soviet Union, were influential figures within Kennedy's administration. Led by individuals such as Secretary of Defense Robert McNamara and Chairman of the Joint Chiefs of Staff General Maxwell Taylor, the hawks advocated for a military solution to the crises in

Cuba. They saw the Bay of Pigs invasion as an opportunity to eliminate the communist threat in the Western Hemisphere and restore American credibility after the perceived failure of the Eisenhower administration. Their advice to Kennedy was to provide air support to the Cuban exiles and escalate the conflict if necessary.

On the other hand, the doves within Kennedy's administration, including Secretary of State Dean Rusk and Attorney General Robert Kennedy, favored a more cautious and diplomatic approach. They were skeptical of the effectiveness of military intervention and feared the potential consequences of an all-out war with the Soviet Union. The doves believed that negotiations and diplomacy were the most viable options to resolve the crises peacefully.

The clash between these two factions created a significant internal struggle within the administration. Kennedy, known for his ability to listen to conflicting viewpoints, found himself torn between the hawkish calls for military action and the dovish pleas for restraint. Ultimately, he pursued a middle ground, carefully considering the advice from both sides but making the final decisions himself.

Understanding the influence of hawks and doves within the administration is essential not only in comprehending Kennedy's decision-making but also in analyzing the public perception of his handling of these crises. The media played a crucial role in shaping public opinion, often portraying Kennedy as indecisive or weak in the face of Soviet aggression. However, historians can now recognize the complex balancing act that Kennedy had to navigate, taking into account the global balance of power and the potential for nuclear war.

In conclusion, the influence of hawks and doves within Kennedy's administration was a significant factor in shaping his decisions during the Bay of Pigs invasion and the Cuban Missile Crisis. Their contrasting perspectives on military intervention and diplomacy created internal tensions, which Kennedy had to navigate carefully. Understanding this dynamic is crucial in comprehending the significance of these events in shaping the global balance of power during the Cold War.

External Pressure and Domestic Political Concerns

The Bay of Pigs invasion and the Cuban Missile Crisis were two critical turning points in the Cold War that shaped the global balance of power. These events were not only influenced by the intense Cold War politics of the time, but also by external pressures and domestic political concerns faced by President John F. Kennedy.

Kennedy's decision-making during the Bay of Pigs invasion was greatly influenced by external pressures. The invasion, which aimed to overthrow Fidel Castro's communist regime in Cuba, was initially planned by the Central Intelligence Agency (CIA) under the Eisenhower administration. However, Kennedy inherited this operation and faced immense pressure to support it from the anti-Castro Cuban exile community and high-ranking officials in his administration. The fear of appearing weak against communism also put pressure on Kennedy to approve the invasion, even though he had reservations about its chances of success.

Furthermore, domestic political concerns played a significant role in shaping Kennedy's decisions during both the Bay of Pigs invasion and the Cuban Missile Crisis. Kennedy was aware that his presidency was still in its early stages and that a failure in Cuba could damage his political reputation. He faced pressure from hawks in his administration who advocated for a more aggressive approach towards Cuba. At the same time, he had to navigate the delicate balance between avoiding nuclear war with the Soviet Union and maintaining a strong stance against communism.

The public perception of Kennedy's handling of these crises was also influenced by external pressures and domestic political concerns. The failure of the Bay of Pigs invasion was seen as a major setback for the Kennedy administration, leading to questions about his leadership and decision-making abilities. However, Kennedy's handling of the Cuban Missile Crisis, where he successfully negotiated the removal of Soviet missiles from Cuba without resorting to military action, was widely applauded.

The role of the media in shaping public opinion during these events cannot be overlooked. The media played a crucial role in disseminating information and shaping public perception. The failure of the Bay of Pigs invasion was heavily covered by the media, leading to a negative portrayal of Kennedy's administration. Conversely, the media portrayed Kennedy as a strong and decisive leader during the Cuban Missile Crisis, which helped bolster his public image.

In conclusion, the external pressures and domestic political concerns faced by President Kennedy greatly influenced his decision-making during the Bay of Pigs invasion and the Cuban Missile Crisis. The public perception of his handling of these crises, shaped by the media, also played a significant role. These events had a profound impact on the global balance of power during the Cold War, highlighting the complexities and challenges faced by leaders during this tumultuous era.

The Role of Military Advisors and Intelligence Agencies

In the context of the Cold War, the role of military advisors and intelligence agencies was paramount in shaping President Kennedy's decision-making during the Bay of Pigs invasion and the Cuban Missile Crisis. These two events were turning points in the Cold War, and their repercussions had a profound impact on global politics and the balance of power.

During the Bay of Pigs invasion, the failure of Kennedy's decision-making process was partly due to the flawed advice he received from his military advisors. The invasion, initially planned as a covert operation to overthrow Fidel Castro's regime, quickly turned into a disaster. The CIA and military advisors had underestimated the Cuban military's capabilities, resulting in the capture and death of numerous American-backed Cuban exiles. This failure highlighted the need for more accurate intelligence and better coordination between intelligence agencies and military advisors.

The Cuban Missile Crisis, occurring just a year later, showcased the crucial role of intelligence agencies in preventing a potential nuclear war. The discovery of Soviet missile installations in Cuba by American intelligence agencies was a pivotal moment in the crisis. The intelligence gathered allowed President Kennedy to make informed decisions and respond with a naval blockade, demanding the removal of the missiles. The CIA's photographic evidence provided undeniable proof of Soviet aggression and helped shape public opinion in favor of the president's actions.

The public perception of Kennedy's handling of both the Bay of Pigs invasion and the Cuban Missile Crisis was heavily influenced by the media. The media played a significant role in shaping public opinion, highlighting the failures of the Bay of Pigs invasion and, later, portraying Kennedy as a strong and decisive leader during the Cuban Missile Crisis. The media's portrayal of Kennedy's handling of these events ultimately influenced his popularity and political standing both domestically and internationally.

These turning points, the Bay of Pigs invasion and the Cuban Missile Crisis, had a profound impact on the global balance of power during the Cold War. The failure of the Bay of Pigs invasion weakened American credibility and emboldened the Soviet Union. It also led

Kennedy to reevaluate his approach to foreign policy and the Cold War, ultimately leading to a more cautious and measured approach in the future. The Cuban Missile Crisis, on the other hand, showcased American resolve and determination to prevent the spread of communism in the Western Hemisphere. It solidified the United States' position as the global superpower and demonstrated the importance of intelligence agencies in preventing catastrophic conflicts.

In conclusion, the role of military advisors and intelligence agencies was instrumental in shaping President Kennedy's decision-making during the Bay of Pigs invasion and the Cuban Missile Crisis. The failures and successes of these events had a profound impact on global politics, the public perception of Kennedy's leadership, and the balance of power during the Cold War. Understanding the significance of these events and the role of military advisors and intelligence agencies is crucial for historians analyzing this critical period in history.

Chapter 3: The Public Perception of Kennedy's Handling of the Bay of Pigs Invasion and the Cuban Missile Crisis

Initial Public Reaction to the Bay of Pigs Invasion

The Bay of Pigs invasion in April 1961 marked a pivotal moment in the early years of the Cold War and had profound implications for the Kennedy administration, the United States, and the global balance of power. As historians, it is crucial to understand the initial public reaction to this event, as it provides valuable insights into the perception and understanding of the Bay of Pigs invasion and its implications.

The American public's response to the invasion was multifaceted, reflecting the complexity of the situation. On one hand, there was initial support and optimism for the operation, fueled by the prevailing anti-communist sentiment of the time. Many Americans saw the intervention in Cuba as a necessary step to counter the spread of communism in the Western Hemisphere. President Kennedy's promise to rid Cuba of Fidel Castro's regime resonated with a significant portion of the population.

However, as news of the invasion's failure began to emerge, the public sentiment quickly shifted. The Bay of Pigs invasion proved to be a colossal military and political failure, and the American people were left disillusioned and embarrassed. Kennedy's decision to withhold direct US military intervention and rely on the CIA-trained Cuban exiles was widely criticized. The public perception of the president's handling of the crisis was one of incompetence and poor judgment.

The media played a crucial role in shaping public opinion during this period. Journalists seized upon the failure of the invasion, highlighting the lack of planning and the flawed execution. The media's portrayal of the Bay of Pigs invasion as a fiasco further eroded public confidence in the Kennedy administration's ability to handle the Cold War challenges. The event became a turning point in the perception of Kennedy's presidency, with many questioning his leadership and decision-making abilities.

Moreover, the Bay of Pigs invasion and its subsequent fallout had far-reaching implications for the global balance of power. The failure of the invasion emboldened the Soviet Union and Fidel Castro, leading to the Cuban Missile Crisis just one year later. The event highlighted the dangerous brinkmanship and nuclear standoff between the superpowers, bringing the world to the brink of nuclear war. The Bay of Pigs invasion and the subsequent Cuban Missile Crisis underscored the significance of Cold War politics in shaping Kennedy's decision-making and the global geopolitical landscape.

In conclusion, the initial public reaction to the Bay of Pigs invasion reflected the optimism and initial support followed by disillusionment and criticism. The media played a crucial role in shaping this perception, while the event itself had significant implications for the global balance of power during the Cold War. Understanding the public's response to the invasion is essential in comprehending the broader historical significance of the Bay of Pigs and the subsequent Cuban Missile Crisis.

The Perception of a Failed Operation

In the annals of Cold War history, few events loom as large as the Bay of Pigs invasion and the Cuban Missile Crisis. These two pivotal moments, separated by a mere year, not only shaped the course of the Cold War but also left an indelible mark on the legacy of President John F. Kennedy. However, it is the perception of these events that has truly shaped our understanding of Kennedy's decision-making and the global balance of power during this critical period.

Kennedy's diluted Bay of Pigs invasion, which took place in April 1961, became a turning point in the Cold War. Intended as a covert operation to overthrow Fidel Castro's communist regime in Cuba, it quickly turned into a catastrophic failure. The invasion forces were ill-prepared and poorly supported, leading to their ultimate defeat. Historians have long debated the reasons behind Kennedy's decision to proceed with such an ill-conceived plan, with many pointing to the influence of Cold War politics. The fear of appearing weak against the spread of communism and the pressure to take bold action against Castro's regime undoubtedly played a significant role in shaping Kennedy's decision-making.

The public perception of Kennedy's handling of the Bay of Pigs invasion was one of disappointment and disillusionment. The American people expected a swift victory and were shocked by the failure of the operation. Kennedy, who had taken full responsibility for the debacle, saw his approval ratings plummet. The media, which played a pivotal role in shaping public opinion, was quick to criticize the administration's handling of the crisis. The perception of a failed operation further heightened tensions during the already tense Cold War era.

However, it was this very perception that ultimately set the stage for the Cuban Missile Crisis. The failed Bay of Pigs invasion led to a sense of urgency within the Kennedy administration. The fear of Soviet influence in Cuba, combined with the public perception of weakness, pushed Kennedy to take a more aggressive stance towards the Soviet Union. The Cuban Missile Crisis, which unfolded in October 1962, brought the world to the brink of nuclear war. It was a direct result of the Cold War politics and the perceived failure of the Bay of Pigs invasion.

The significance of these events in shaping the global balance of power during the Cold War cannot be overstated. The failed Bay of Pigs invasion and the subsequent Cuban Missile Crisis highlighted the dangers of brinkmanship and the need for cautious decision-making in the face of nuclear threats. It also served as a wake-up call to the international community, leading to increased efforts to prevent the escalation of conflicts and the proliferation of nuclear weapons.

In conclusion, the perception of a failed operation has had far-reaching implications in our understanding of Kennedy's decision-making, the role of Cold War politics, the public perception of his handling of the crisis, the influence of the media, and the significance of these events in shaping the global balance of power. The Bay of Pigs invasion and the Cuban Missile Crisis remain defining moments of the Cold War, forever etched in the annals of history.

Questions about Kennedy's Leadership and Competence

Introduction:

In this subchapter, we will delve into the questions surrounding President John F. Kennedy's leadership and competence during two critical events of the Cold War era: the Bay of Pigs invasion and the Cuban Missile Crisis. These events not only had a significant impact on the global balance of power but also shaped Kennedy's decision-making process and public perception of his handling of these crises. By analyzing the role of Cold War politics, the media's influence, and the long-term implications of these events, we can gain a deeper understanding of Kennedy's leadership and competence during these tumultuous times.

Kennedy's Diluted Bay of Pigs Invasion Created One Year Later the Cuban Missile Crisis:

One of the fundamental questions asked by historians is how Kennedy's initial failure in the Bay of Pigs invasion contributed to the subsequent Cuban Missile Crisis. By examining the decision-making process behind the invasion and the consequences of its failure, we can evaluate Kennedy's leadership and competence in handling this pivotal moment in Cold War history.

The Role of Cold War Politics in Shaping Kennedy's Decision-making:

Another area of inquiry focuses on the influence of Cold War politics on Kennedy's decision-making during both the Bay of Pigs invasion and the Cuban Missile Crisis. Understanding the broader geopolitical context and the pressures faced by Kennedy can shed light on his leadership abilities and the factors that shaped his responses to these crises.

The Public Perception of Kennedy's Handling of the Bay of Pigs Invasion and the Cuban Missile Crisis:

Public perception plays a crucial role in assessing a leader's competence. By analyzing contemporary accounts and public opinion polls, we can examine how Kennedy's handling of the Bay of Pigs invasion and the Cuban Missile Crisis was perceived by the American people. This will provide insight into how his leadership and decision-making were judged at the time.

The Role of the Media in Shaping Public Opinion:

The media's role in shaping public opinion cannot be underestimated, particularly during times of crisis. Examining how the media reported on and interpreted the events of the Bay of Pigs invasion and the

Cuban Missile Crisis will offer valuable insights into how Kennedy's leadership and competence were portrayed to the public.

The Significance of the Bay of Pigs Invasion and the Cuban Missile Crisis in Shaping the Global Balance of Power:

Finally, we will explore the long-term implications of these events on the global balance of power during the Cold War. By assessing the consequences of Kennedy's decisions, we can evaluate his leadership and competence in the broader context of Cold War dynamics.

Conclusion:

In this subchapter, we have explored the questions surrounding Kennedy's leadership and competence during the Bay of Pigs invasion and the Cuban Missile Crisis. By examining the influence of Cold War politics, the media's role in shaping public opinion, and the long-term significance of these events, we can gain a comprehensive understanding of Kennedy's decision-making and its impact on the global balance of power during the Cold War.

The Impact on Kennedy's Approval Ratings

One of the most significant aspects of President John F. Kennedy's presidency was the impact that the Bay of Pigs invasion and the Cuban Missile Crisis had on his approval ratings. These two events played a crucial role in shaping public opinion of Kennedy's decision-making and leadership during the Cold War era.

Kennedy's Diluted Bay of Pigs Invasion Created One Year Later the Cuban Missile Crisis

The Bay of Pigs invasion, which took place in April 1961, was a failed attempt by the United States to overthrow the communist regime of Fidel Castro in Cuba. The invasion, initially planned by the Central

Intelligence Agency (CIA) during the Eisenhower administration, was ultimately carried out under Kennedy's presidency. However, Kennedy decided to scale back the invasion plan, which led to the failure of the mission and a significant loss of American prestige.

The failure of the Bay of Pigs invasion had a profound impact on Kennedy's approval ratings. Many Americans viewed it as a botched operation and questioned Kennedy's ability to handle Cold War crises effectively. This perception was soon reinforced by the subsequent Cuban Missile Crisis.

The Role of Cold War Politics in Shaping Kennedy's Decision-Making

The Bay of Pigs invasion and the Cuban Missile Crisis were both heavily influenced by the political dynamics of the Cold War. Kennedy was under immense pressure to demonstrate American strength and resolve in the face of Soviet expansionism. The fear of communist influence spreading throughout the Western Hemisphere, particularly in Latin America, played a significant role in shaping Kennedy's decision-making during these two events.

The Public Perception of Kennedy's Handling of the Bay of Pigs Invasion and the Cuban Missile Crisis

The public perception of Kennedy's handling of the Bay of Pigs invasion and the Cuban Missile Crisis had a direct impact on his approval ratings. Initially, Kennedy received some criticism for the failure of the Bay of Pigs invasion. However, his handling of the Cuban Missile Crisis, which occurred in October 1962, helped to restore public confidence in his leadership.

Kennedy's calm and measured approach during the Cuban Missile Crisis, coupled with his successful resolution of the crisis through a diplomatic agreement with Soviet leader Nikita Khrushchev, boosted his approval ratings significantly. The American public saw Kennedy as a strong and decisive leader who was capable of navigating through the dangerous waters of the Cold War.

The Role of the Media in Shaping Public Opinion

The media played a crucial role in shaping public opinion during both the Bay of Pigs invasion and the Cuban Missile Crisis. The media coverage of the Bay of Pigs invasion highlighted the failure of the operation and contributed to the negative perception of Kennedy's decision-making. However, during the Cuban Missile Crisis, the media portrayed Kennedy as a resolute and competent leader, which helped to improve his approval ratings.

The Significance of the Bay of Pigs Invasion and the Cuban Missile Crisis in Shaping the Global Balance of Power

The Bay of Pigs invasion and the Cuban Missile Crisis had a significant impact on the global balance of power during the Cold War. The failure of the Bay of Pigs invasion allowed Castro to solidify his grip on power in Cuba and establish a closer alliance with the Soviet Union. This, in turn, led to the Cuban Missile Crisis, which brought the world to the brink of nuclear war. The successful resolution of the crisis by Kennedy helped to maintain the delicate balance of power between the United States and the Soviet Union.

In conclusion, the Bay of Pigs invasion and the Cuban Missile Crisis had a profound impact on Kennedy's approval ratings. These events shaped public perception of his decision-making and leadership during the Cold War era. The media played a crucial role in shaping public opinion, while the significance of these events in shaping the global balance of power cannot be overstated. Understanding the impact of these events is crucial in comprehending Kennedy's role in the Cold War and his place in history.

The Cuban Missile Crisis and Public Opinion

Throughout history, public opinion has played a crucial role in shaping the course of events and influencing decision-making processes. The Cuban Missile Crisis, a pivotal moment in the Cold War, was no exception. This subchapter explores the intricate relationship between the crisis and public opinion, shedding light on the various factors that influenced the public perception of President John F. Kennedy's actions during this critical period.

One of the key aspects to consider when examining the Cuban Missile Crisis is how it was intricately connected to the Bay of Pigs invasion, which had taken place a year earlier. Kennedy's diluted Bay of Pigs invasion, a failed attempt to overthrow Fidel Castro's regime, had far-reaching consequences. It not only served as a catalyst for the subsequent Soviet deployment of missiles to Cuba but also influenced Kennedy's decision-making during the crisis.

Cold War politics also played a significant role in shaping Kennedy's response to the crisis. The escalating tensions between the United States and the Soviet Union had created a climate of fear and anxiety, heightening the stakes of the crisis. Kennedy's decisions were influenced by the desire to maintain U.S. credibility and deter further Soviet aggression, while avoiding a potentially catastrophic nuclear war.

Public perception of Kennedy's handling of both the Bay of Pigs invasion and the Cuban Missile Crisis was mixed. While some praised his resolve and leadership, others criticized his initial mishandling of the Bay of Pigs invasion, leading to questions about his ability to effectively manage the crisis. The public's perception was further shaped by the media, which played a crucial role in disseminating information and shaping public opinion.

The media's coverage of the crisis was instrumental in shaping public opinion. Newspapers, television, and radio broadcasts provided constant updates and analysis, effectively informing the public and shaping their understanding of the situation. The media's interpretation of events, coupled with the government's efforts to manage the narrative, influenced the public's perception of Kennedy's actions during this critical period.

Ultimately, the significance of the Bay of Pigs invasion and the Cuban Missile Crisis cannot be understated in shaping the global balance of power during the Cold War. The crisis brought the world to the brink of nuclear war and highlighted the need for diplomacy and international cooperation. It also demonstrated the importance of public opinion in influencing decision-making processes and shaping the course of history.

In conclusion, the Cuban Missile Crisis and public opinion are interconnected in numerous ways. The crisis was influenced by the Bay of Pigs invasion and Cold War politics, while public perception was shaped by the media's coverage and the government's narrative. Understanding the role of public opinion in this historical event is crucial for historians seeking to comprehend the complexities of Kennedy's decisions and the global impact of the crisis within the context of the Cold War.

The Heightened Sense of Fear and Anxiety

In the annals of history, few events have captured the collective imagination and instilled a heightened sense of fear and anxiety like the Bay of Pigs invasion and the Cuban Missile Crisis. These two pivotal moments in the Cold War era, both intricately linked to President John F. Kennedy's decisions, continue to captivate historians and scholars to this day.

Kennedy's Diluted Bay of Pigs Invasion Created One Year Later the Cuban Missile Crisis

The failed Bay of Pigs invasion, launched in April 1961, set the stage for the Cuban Missile Crisis a year later. Kennedy's decision to support a clandestine invasion by Cuban exiles was fraught with miscalculations and missteps. The botched attempt not only resulted in a crushing defeat but also served as a powerful symbol of American weakness. It emboldened Soviet Premier Nikita Khrushchev to push further into the Western Hemisphere, ultimately leading to the placement of nuclear missiles on Cuban soil.

The Role of Cold War Politics in Shaping Kennedy's Decision-Making

Cold War politics played a pivotal role in shaping Kennedy's decision-making during these crises. Faced with the growing threat of communism, Kennedy sought to demonstrate American resolve and preserve the credibility of the United States as a global superpower. However, the delicate balance between containment and escalation forced Kennedy to navigate treacherous waters, often under immense pressure from his advisors and the military-industrial complex.

The Public Perception of Kennedy's Handling of the Crises

The public perception of Kennedy's handling of the Bay of Pigs invasion and the Cuban Missile Crisis was a fascinating study in the power of image and narrative. Initially hailed as a young and charismatic leader, Kennedy's reputation took a hit following the failed invasion. However, his adept crisis management during the Cuban Missile Crisis helped restore public confidence and solidify his legacy as a steady-handed leader.

The Role of Media in Shaping Public Opinion

The media played a crucial role in shaping public opinion during these crises. The advent of television brought the realities of war and the specter of nuclear annihilation directly into people's living rooms. The vivid images and compelling narratives conveyed by the media had a profound impact on public sentiment, sometimes influencing the course of events and the subsequent decision-making of political leaders.

The Significance of the Crises in Shaping the Global Balance of Power

The Bay of Pigs invasion and the Cuban Missile Crisis were pivotal moments that reshaped the global balance of power during the Cold War. The events underscored the dangers of brinkmanship and highlighted the need for diplomacy and effective crisis management. They also served as a catalyst for nuclear arms control and détente between the United States and the Soviet Union, setting the stage for future negotiations and shaping the course of the Cold War.

In conclusion, the heightened sense of fear and anxiety surrounding the Bay of Pigs invasion and the Cuban Missile Crisis reverberated throughout history. The decisions made by President Kennedy, influenced by Cold War politics, shaped the perceptions of both the American public and the global community. The media played a significant role in shaping public opinion, while the consequences of these crises had far-reaching implications for the balance of power during the Cold War.

Public Support for Kennedy's Handling of the Crisis

One of the most remarkable aspects of President John F. Kennedy's handling of the Bay of Pigs invasion and the Cuban Missile Crisis was the overwhelming support he received from the American public. Despite the initial failure of the Bay of Pigs invasion, Kennedy's leadership and decision-making during the crisis garnered widespread approval and admiration from the American people.

Kennedy's ability to effectively communicate with the American public played a crucial role in gaining their support. Through his televised addresses and press conferences, Kennedy presented himself as a calm and confident leader, assuring the nation that he was in control of the situation. His ability to convey a sense of purpose and determination in dealing with the crisis resonated with the American people, who saw him as a strong and capable leader in the face of a grave threat.

The role of the media in shaping public opinion cannot be understated. The media played a significant role in presenting Kennedy's handling of the crisis to the American public. Journalists and reporters praised Kennedy's cool-headedness and strategic decision-making, portraying him as a resolute leader who was able to navigate the treacherous waters of the Cold War. Their positive coverage of Kennedy's actions during the crisis helped to shape public opinion and generate support for his handling of the situation.

Furthermore, the significance of the Bay of Pigs invasion and the Cuban Missile Crisis in shaping the global balance of power during the Cold War cannot be underestimated. Kennedy's firm stance against the Soviet Union's deployment of nuclear missiles in Cuba demonstrated his commitment to protecting American interests and deterring aggression. This bold and decisive action helped to restore the confidence of the American public in their government's ability to confront and contain the communist threat.

In conclusion, Kennedy's handling of the Bay of Pigs invasion and the Cuban Missile Crisis received overwhelming public support. Through his effective communication with the American people and the positive portrayal by the media, Kennedy was able to rally public opinion and garner support for his decisions. The significance of these crises in shaping the global balance of power during the Cold War further solidified Kennedy's reputation as a strong and capable leader. Historians continue to study and analyze Kennedy's decision-making during these turning points of the Cold War, recognizing the public support he received as a testament to his leadership skills and ability to navigate through challenging times.

The Perception of Diplomatic Success and Avoidance of Nuclear War

Throughout history, diplomatic success has often been measured by a nation's ability to navigate through crises and avoid devastating conflicts. In the context of the Cold War, President John F. Kennedy's decisions during the Bay of Pigs invasion and the Cuban Missile Crisis were pivotal moments that shaped the global balance of power and the perception of his leadership.

Kennedy's diluted Bay of Pigs invasion, which took place in April 1961, had significant implications for the events that unfolded one year later during the Cuban Missile Crisis. The failed invasion not only highlighted the limitations of American power but also provided valuable lessons to Kennedy and his advisors. The invasion's failure made Kennedy more cautious and aware of the potential consequences of aggressive actions against the Soviet Union.

The role of Cold War politics cannot be understated in understanding Kennedy's decision-making during these crises. The United States and the Soviet Union were locked in a bitter struggle for global dominance, and any misstep by either side could have escalated into a nuclear war. Kennedy's decisions were influenced by the need to maintain the delicate balance of power while preventing the situation from spiraling out of control.

The public perception of Kennedy's handling of the Bay of Pigs invasion and the Cuban Missile Crisis played a crucial role in shaping his legacy. Initially, the Bay of Pigs invasion was viewed as a failure, with many questioning Kennedy's leadership abilities. However, his handling of the Cuban Missile Crisis, where he successfully navigated a dangerous standoff with the Soviets, transformed public opinion and bolstered his image as a strong and capable leader.

The media played a significant role in shaping public opinion during these crises. The coverage of the events by the press influenced public perception and impacted the government's decision-making process. The media's portrayal of Kennedy's actions during the crises further highlighted the importance of diplomatic success and avoidance of nuclear war in the eyes of the public.

Ultimately, the Bay of Pigs invasion and the Cuban Missile Crisis had far-reaching consequences in shaping the global balance of power during the Cold War. Kennedy's ability to avoid a nuclear conflict with the Soviet Union was seen as a diplomatic success, and it solidified the perception of his leadership during this critical period. These events served as a turning point, leading to a reevaluation of U.S. foreign policy and a renewed emphasis on diplomacy to prevent nuclear war.

In conclusion, the perception of diplomatic success and the avoidance of nuclear war were paramount in understanding the significance of Kennedy's decisions during the Bay of Pigs invasion and the Cuban Missile Crisis. These events shaped global power dynamics, influenced public opinion, and highlighted the importance of diplomatic finesse in avoiding catastrophic conflicts. The lessons learned from these crises continue to resonate in the study of Cold War history and serve as reminders of the fragility of international relations.

Historical Assessment and Changing Public Opinion

In the annals of Cold War history, few events have had such a profound impact on global politics as the Bay of Pigs invasion and the Cuban Missile Crisis. These two pivotal moments, both intimately linked to President John F. Kennedy's decision-making, played a crucial role in shaping the dynamics of the Cold War and reshaping public opinion.

Kennedy's Diluted Bay of Pigs Invasion Created One Year Later the Cuban Missile Crisis

The Bay of Pigs invasion, launched in April 1961, was initially intended to overthrow Fidel Castro's communist regime in Cuba. However, Kennedy's decision to scale down the invasion force and not provide air support ultimately led to its failure. This diluted operation had far-reaching consequences, as it not only emboldened Castro but also increased Soviet influence in the region. In fact, it was the Bay of Pigs failure that set the stage for the Cuban Missile Crisis, which erupted just a year later.

The Role of Cold War Politics in Shaping Kennedy's Decision-Making

Cold War politics heavily influenced Kennedy's decision-making during both the Bay of Pigs invasion and the Cuban Missile Crisis. The United States was engaged in a global struggle for influence with the Soviet Union, and Kennedy was acutely aware of the need to project American strength and resolve. However, the complexities of the Cold War also presented challenges, with the fear of escalating tensions and the potential for nuclear war looming over every decision.

The Public Perception of Kennedy's Handling of the Bay of Pigs Invasion and the Cuban Missile Crisis

Public opinion played a significant role in how Kennedy's handling of the Bay of Pigs invasion and the Cuban Missile Crisis was perceived. Initially, the failure of the Bay of Pigs invasion was a blow to Kennedy's reputation, with critics accusing him of weakness and indecisiveness. However, his handling of the Cuban Missile Crisis, particularly his measured response and successful negotiation with Soviet Premier Nikita Khrushchev, boosted his image and solidified his reputation as a capable leader.

The Role of the Media in Shaping Public Opinion

During these critical moments, the media played a crucial role in shaping public opinion. The Bay of Pigs invasion was extensively covered, with the media highlighting the failures of the operation and questioning Kennedy's leadership. However, during the Cuban Missile Crisis, the media portrayed Kennedy as a resolute and decisive leader, rallying support for his actions and emphasizing the gravity of the situation.

The Significance of the Bay of Pigs Invasion and the Cuban Missile Crisis in Shaping the Global Balance of Power

Both the Bay of Pigs invasion and the Cuban Missile Crisis had profound implications for the global balance of power during the Cold War. The Bay of Pigs failure allowed the Soviet Union to solidify its presence in Cuba, increasing tensions and setting the stage for the Cuban Missile Crisis. This crisis brought the world to the brink of nuclear war and ultimately led to a reevaluation of Cold War strategies and a more cautious approach to superpower relations.

In conclusion, the Bay of Pigs invasion and the Cuban Missile Crisis were turning points in the Cold War, with lasting consequences for global politics. Kennedy's decision-making, public opinion, media coverage, and the shifting balance of power all played crucial roles in shaping the outcomes and the subsequent trajectory of the Cold War. Understanding the historical assessment and changing public opinion of these events provides valuable insights into this critical period in history.

Reevaluating Kennedy's Decisions in Light of New Information

Introduction:

In the annals of history, few events have been as pivotal and consequential as the Bay of Pigs invasion and the Cuban Missile Crisis during the Cold War era. These incidents not only brought the world to the brink of nuclear war but also shaped the global balance of power for years to come. As historians, it is our duty to continuously reevaluate and reassess the decisions made by key figures, such as President John F. Kennedy, in light of new information that emerges over time. By doing so, we can gain a more nuanced understanding of the complex factors at play during these critical turning points.

Kennedy's Diluted Bay of Pigs Invasion Created One Year Later the Cuban Missile Crisis:

One of the key aspects that historians should reevaluate is the connection between Kennedy's diluted Bay of Pigs invasion and the subsequent Cuban Missile Crisis. While initially seen as separate events, recent research suggests a direct causal link between these two incidents. By examining new evidence, such as declassified documents and firsthand accounts, we can unearth the intricate web of Cold War politics that influenced Kennedy's decision-making.

The Role of Cold War Politics in Shaping Kennedy's Decision-Making:

Kennedy's decisions during the Bay of Pigs invasion and the Cuban Missile Crisis were heavily influenced by the prevailing Cold War politics of the time. Reevaluating these decisions in light of new information allows us to delve deeper into the geopolitical considerations, power dynamics, and ideological struggles that shaped Kennedy's approach. By understanding these factors, we can gain a more comprehensive understanding of the motivations behind his actions.

The Public Perception of Kennedy's Handling:

Another crucial aspect to consider is the public perception of Kennedy's handling of these crises. While Kennedy's public image was initially tarnished by the perceived failure of the Bay of Pigs invasion, his handling of the Cuban Missile Crisis was widely hailed as a success.

Reevaluating public sentiment through the lens of new information and primary sources can provide insights into the factors that influenced public opinion and the role of the media in shaping it.

The Role of the Media in Shaping Public Opinion:

The media played a significant role in shaping public opinion during the Bay of Pigs invasion and the Cuban Missile Crisis. By examining the media's portrayal of these events and its impact on public sentiment, historians can gain a deeper understanding of the influence wielded by the media during critical moments in history. Reevaluating the media's role can shed light on the interplay between information dissemination, public perception, and the decision-making of key figures.

The Significance of the Bay of Pigs Invasion and the Cuban Missile Crisis:

Lastly, it is vital to reevaluate the significance of the Bay of Pigs invasion and the Cuban Missile Crisis in shaping the global balance of power during the Cold War. These events not only heightened tensions between the United States and the Soviet Union but also fundamentally altered the course of history. By examining new information and reassessing their impact, historians can offer fresh insights into how these events influenced the trajectory of the Cold War and its subsequent ramifications on global politics.

Conclusion:

Reevaluating Kennedy's decisions in light of new information is crucial for historians seeking a comprehensive understanding of the Bay of Pigs invasion and the Cuban Missile Crisis. By examining the connection between these events, the role of Cold War politics, public perception, media influence, and the global balance of power, we can gain a more nuanced understanding of these critical turning points in history. Through this ongoing reassessment, we can continue to illuminate the complex factors that shaped Kennedy's decision-making and the broader implications of these events on the Cold War era.

The Influence of Historical Narratives and Revisionist Interpretations

In the realm of historical analysis, the influence of historical narratives and revisionist interpretations cannot be overstated. These narratives shape the way we perceive and understand past events, often leading to different interpretations and conclusions. Within the context of the Cold War, two pivotal events that have garnered significant attention and debate are Kennedy's decisions in the Bay of Pigs invasion and the Cuban Missile Crisis. These events not only shaped the course of the Cold War but also influenced Kennedy's decision-making and public perception.

Kennedy's Diluted Bay of Pigs Invasion Created One Year Later the Cuban Missile Crisis

One of the key arguments put forth by historians is the direct link between Kennedy's diluted Bay of Pigs invasion and the subsequent Cuban Missile Crisis. It is suggested that the failed invasion in 1961 created a sense of vulnerability and humiliation for the United States, emboldening Soviet Premier Nikita Khrushchev to install nuclear missiles in Cuba in 1962. This interpretation emphasizes the importance of understanding the interconnectedness of these events and their long-term consequences.

The Role of Cold War Politics in Shaping Kennedy's Decision-Making

Cold War politics played a significant role in shaping Kennedy's decision-making during both the Bay of Pigs invasion and the Cuban Missile Crisis. Kennedy faced immense pressure to appear strong and resolute in the face of Soviet aggression. This led him to make decisions that were influenced by the larger geopolitical context of the Cold

War, rather than solely based on the specific circumstances of each event. Understanding the influence of Cold War politics on Kennedy's decision-making is crucial in comprehending the complexity of these historical moments.

The Public Perception of Kennedy's Handling of the Bay of Pigs Invasion and the Cuban Missile Crisis

The public perception of Kennedy's handling of the Bay of Pigs invasion and the Cuban Missile Crisis varied greatly. While some praised his leadership and crisis management skills, others criticized his initial missteps and perceived weaknesses. This differing public perception highlights the importance of historical narratives and how they shape our understanding and evaluation of past events. It also underscores the role of the media in shaping public opinion during these crises.

The Role of the Media in Shaping Public Opinion

The media played a crucial role in shaping public opinion during the Bay of Pigs invasion and the Cuban Missile Crisis. Through their reporting, journalists influenced the way these events were understood and perceived by the public. The media's portrayal of Kennedy's actions, both positive and negative, contributed to the formation of historical narratives surrounding these events. Recognizing the influence of the media is essential to gaining a comprehensive understanding of how these historical moments were interpreted at the time.

The Significance of the Bay of Pigs Invasion and the Cuban Missile Crisis in Shaping the Global Balance of Power

Lastly, it is crucial to acknowledge the significance of the Bay of Pigs invasion and the Cuban Missile Crisis in shaping the global balance of power during the Cold War. These events heightened tensions between the United States and the Soviet Union, bringing the world to the brink of nuclear war. The lessons learned from these crises influenced subsequent policies and strategies in the Cold War era and beyond. Understanding their significance within the larger context of the global balance of power provides valuable insights into the broader historical narrative of the Cold War.

In conclusion, the influence of historical narratives and revisionist interpretations is central to our understanding of the Bay of Pigs invasion and the Cuban Missile Crisis. By examining Kennedy's decisions, the role of Cold War politics, public perception, media influence, and the significance of these events in shaping the global balance of power, historians can gain a comprehensive understanding of these pivotal moments in Cold War history.

The Lasting Impact on Kennedy's Legacy and Public Perception

The events of the Bay of Pigs invasion and the Cuban Missile Crisis had a profound and lasting impact on President John F. Kennedy's legacy and the public's perception of him. These two pivotal moments during the Cold War shaped not only the course of Kennedy's presidency but also the global balance of power.

Kennedy's Diluted Bay of Pigs Invasion Created One Year Later the Cuban Missile Crisis

The failed Bay of Pigs invasion in April 1961 set the stage for the Cuban Missile Crisis in October 1962. The botched CIA-led operation to overthrow Fidel Castro's regime in Cuba tarnished Kennedy's credibility and raised doubts about his ability to handle Cold War challenges. The Bay of Pigs invasion was seen as a major setback for the United States, and it emboldened the Soviet Union to test Kennedy's resolve.

The Role of Cold War Politics in Shaping Kennedy's Decision-Making

During both the Bay of Pigs invasion and the Cuban Missile Crisis, Kennedy's decisions were heavily influenced by the Cold War politics of the time. The fear of communist expansion and the desire to maintain American credibility in the face of Soviet aggression guided Kennedy's actions. The Bay of Pigs invasion, for instance, was driven by a desire to contain communism in the Western Hemisphere and prevent the spread of Soviet influence.

The Public Perception of Kennedy's Handling of the Crises

Kennedy's handling of the Bay of Pigs invasion and the Cuban Missile Crisis evoked mixed reactions from the American public. While his response to the Cuban Missile Crisis was widely praised as a display of strong leadership and strategic acumen, the failure of the Bay of Pigs invasion led to criticism and questions about his decision-making abilities. Despite this setback, Kennedy's handling of the subsequent crisis helped rehabilitate his image and bolstered public support for his administration.

The Role of the Media in Shaping Public Opinion

The media played a crucial role in shaping public opinion during both the Bay of Pigs invasion and the Cuban Missile Crisis. The invasion was heavily covered by the press, and the images of captured American-backed rebels and the subsequent fallout damaged Kennedy's reputation. During the Cuban Missile Crisis, however, the media largely supported Kennedy's actions and helped foster a sense of unity and purpose among the American people.

The Significance of the Crises in Shaping the Global Balance of Power

The Bay of Pigs invasion and the Cuban Missile Crisis were pivotal moments in the Cold War and had far-reaching implications for the global balance of power. The events highlighted the dangerous brinkmanship between the United States and the Soviet Union and underscored the need for effective communication and diplomacy to prevent a nuclear war. The resolution of the Cuban Missile Crisis also marked a turning point in the Cold War, as both sides recognized the dangers of escalation and took steps towards détente.

In conclusion, the Bay of Pigs invasion and the Cuban Missile Crisis had a lasting impact on Kennedy's legacy and the public's perception of him. These events shaped his decision-making, influenced public opinion, and played a significant role in shaping the global balance of power during the Cold War. The consequences of these crises continue to be studied and analyzed by historians, providing valuable insights into the challenges and complexities of international relations during this tumultuous period.

Chapter 4: The Role of the Media in Shaping Public Opinion during the Bay of Pigs Invasion and the Cuban Missile Crisis

The Media's Coverage of the Bay of Pigs Invasion

Title: The Media's Coverage of the Bay of Pigs Invasion: Shaping Public Opinion and Influencing Global Balance of Power during the Cold War

Introduction:

The media's coverage of the Bay of Pigs Invasion and the subsequent Cuban Missile Crisis played a pivotal role in shaping public opinion and influencing the global balance of power during the Cold War. This subchapter explores the impact of the media's coverage on these significant turning points in history, highlighting the role of Cold War politics in Kennedy's decision-making and the public perception of his handling of these crises.

Kennedy's Diluted Bay of Pigs Invasion Created One Year Later the Cuban Missile Crisis:

The media's coverage of the Bay of Pigs Invasion shed light on Kennedy's decision-making process and the subsequent consequences. By examining the diluted nature of the invasion, historians can understand how Kennedy's cautious approach inadvertently paved the way for the Cuban Missile Crisis. The media's coverage brought attention to the failed invasion, exposing the flaws in the administration's plan and highlighting the need for a more assertive stance against communist expansion.

The Role of Cold War Politics in Shaping Kennedy's Decision-Making:

Cold War politics played a significant role in shaping Kennedy's decision-making during both the Bay of Pigs Invasion and the Cuban Missile Crisis. The fear of communism and the ideological battle between the United States and the Soviet Union influenced Kennedy's choices. The media's coverage of these events showcased the gravity of the situation, emphasizing the high stakes involved and the need for strong leadership.

The Public Perception of Kennedy's Handling of the Crises:

The media's coverage had a profound impact on public perception of Kennedy's handling of the Bay of Pigs Invasion and the Cuban Missile Crisis. Initially, Kennedy's approval ratings declined due to the perceived failure of the Bay of Pigs Invasion. However, his handling of the Cuban Missile Crisis, which was widely praised by the media, helped restore the public's confidence in his leadership. The media's portrayal of Kennedy's decision-making played a crucial role in shaping public opinion and the overall support for his administration.

The Role of Media in Shaping Public Opinion:

The media played a significant role in shaping public opinion during the Bay of Pigs Invasion and the Cuban Missile Crisis. Through their reporting, journalists influenced public perception, highlighting the risks of inaction and the potential consequences of a nuclear conflict. The media's coverage also exposed the covert operations and secretive nature of these events, leading to increased public scrutiny and demands for transparency.

The Significance of the Crises in Shaping the Global Balance of Power:

Both the Bay of Pigs Invasion and the Cuban Missile Crisis had far-reaching implications for the global balance of power during the

Cold War. The media's coverage brought international attention to these events, underscoring the dangers of nuclear escalation and the importance of diplomatic negotiations. The crises marked a turning point in the Cold War, as the world witnessed the potential catastrophic consequences of superpower confrontation.

Conclusion:

The media's coverage of the Bay of Pigs Invasion and the Cuban Missile Crisis had a profound impact on shaping public opinion, influencing Kennedy's decision-making, and ultimately shaping the global balance of power during the Cold War. Understanding the media's role in these crises is crucial for historians, as it provides valuable insights into the complexities of Cold War politics, the power of public perception, and the significance of these events in shaping the course of history.

The Initial Reporting and Narrative Framing

In the world of history, few events have had such a profound impact on global politics as the Bay of Pigs invasion and the Cuban Missile Crisis. These two episodes not only showcased the complexities of Cold War politics but also highlighted the critical role that President John F. Kennedy played in shaping the outcome of these crises. This subchapter delves into the initial reporting and narrative framing surrounding these events, shedding light on their historical significance and the public perception of Kennedy's decisions.

Kennedy's Diluted Bay of Pigs Invasion Created One Year Later the Cuban Missile Crisis

The initial reporting of the Bay of Pigs invasion was marred by a sense of confusion and failure. The invasion, which aimed to overthrow Fidel Castro's regime in Cuba, ended in disaster due to a lack of proper planning and intelligence. The diluted nature of the invasion plan was a direct result of Kennedy's cautious approach, influenced by concerns about provoking a larger conflict with the Soviet Union. Little did Kennedy know that his restrained response to the Bay of Pigs would set the stage for an even more dangerous standoff a year later - the Cuban Missile Crisis.

The Role of Cold War Politics in Shaping Kennedy's Decision-making

Cold War politics heavily influenced Kennedy's decision-making during both the Bay of Pigs invasion and the Cuban Missile Crisis. The fear of nuclear war and the desire to demonstrate American resolve against communism played a significant role in shaping Kennedy's actions. The subchapter explores the intricate web of alliances, rivalries, and ideologies that informed Kennedy's choices, highlighting how the geopolitical landscape of the Cold War era influenced his decision-making process.

The Public Perception of Kennedy's Handling

The public perception of Kennedy's handling of these crises was a crucial factor in shaping their historical narrative. The subchapter examines how Kennedy's initial admission of responsibility for the failure of the Bay of Pigs invasion, coupled with his later resolve during the Cuban Missile Crisis, affected public opinion. It explores the tension between criticism and admiration, highlighting the complexities of public perception and the lasting impact on Kennedy's legacy.

The Role of the Media in Shaping Public Opinion

The media played a pivotal role in shaping public opinion during the Bay of Pigs invasion and the Cuban Missile Crisis. The subchapter delves into the media's reporting of these events, as well as the narratives they constructed. It analyzes the media's influence on public sentiment, exploring how their portrayal of Kennedy's decision-making impacted the public's perception of these crises.

The Significance in Shaping the Global Balance of Power

Lastly, this subchapter underscores the immense significance of the Bay of Pigs invasion and the Cuban Missile Crisis in shaping the global balance of power during the Cold War. These events heightened tensions between the United States and the Soviet Union, pushing the world to the brink of nuclear war. The subchapter examines how these crises altered the dynamics of the Cold War, ultimately influencing the course of history.

In conclusion, the initial reporting and narrative framing surrounding the Bay of Pigs invasion and the Cuban Missile Crisis played a crucial role in shaping public perception, influencing the global balance of power, and highlighting the complexities of Kennedy's decision-making during the Cold War. Understanding these aspects is vital for historians seeking to comprehend the profound impact of these turning points in the history of the Cold War.

Criticism and Analysis of Kennedy's Decision-Making

In the annals of the Cold War, no two events loom larger than the Bay of Pigs invasion and the Cuban Missile Crisis. These pivotal moments in history, both of which occurred during President John F. Kennedy's tenure, have been subjected to intense scrutiny by historians seeking to understand the decision-making processes that shaped them. This subchapter aims to delve into the criticism and analysis surrounding Kennedy's role in these events, shedding light on the complexities and consequences of his choices.

One of the primary criticisms leveled against Kennedy pertains to the diluted nature of the Bay of Pigs invasion and its impact on the subsequent Cuban Missile Crisis. Historians argue that Kennedy's decision to curtail the initial invasion plan weakened the operation, leading to its ultimate failure. By not providing adequate air support and denying the rebels the necessary resources, Kennedy inadvertently created conditions that emboldened Fidel Castro's regime and set the stage for the Cuban Missile Crisis a year later.

Cold War politics played a significant role in shaping Kennedy's decision-making during both the Bay of Pigs invasion and the Cuban Missile Crisis. The fear of appearing weak in the face of Soviet aggression, coupled with the desire to prevent communism from expanding in the Western Hemisphere, heavily influenced Kennedy's choices. Critics argue that this focus on Cold War politics clouded his judgment and led to flawed decision-making, particularly in the case of the Bay of Pigs invasion.

The public perception of Kennedy's handling of these crises also came under scrutiny. While some praised his resolve and measured approach during the Cuban Missile Crisis, others viewed his handling of the Bay of Pigs invasion as a grave failure. The perception of Kennedy as a strong leader during the Missile Crisis was bolstered by his televised addresses to the nation, which helped shape public opinion and garnered support for his actions. However, the negative fallout from the Bay of Pigs invasion tarnished his reputation and raised doubts about his competency.

The media played a pivotal role in shaping public opinion during both the Bay of Pigs invasion and the Cuban Missile Crisis. Journalistic coverage of these events influenced the way they were perceived domestically and internationally. Critics argue that the media's portrayal of Kennedy's actions during the Bay of Pigs invasion as indecisive and ill-conceived further damaged his reputation, while its coverage of the Missile Crisis painted him as a resolute leader.

Lastly, it is crucial to recognize the significance of these events in shaping the global balance of power during the Cold War. The failure of the Bay of Pigs invasion and the subsequent discovery of Soviet missiles in Cuba heightened tensions between the United States and the Soviet Union, bringing the world to the brink of nuclear war. Kennedy's decisions during these crises had far-reaching implications for the Cold War and underscored the delicate nature of global politics during this era.

In conclusion, the criticism and analysis of Kennedy's decision-making during the Bay of Pigs invasion and the Cuban Missile Crisis reveal the complexities and consequences of his choices. The diluted nature of the Bay of Pigs invasion, the role of Cold War politics, the public perception, the media's influence, and the global significance of these events all contribute to a deeper understanding of this critical period in history. By examining Kennedy's decision-making through these lenses, historians can gain valuable insights into the dynamics that shaped the Cold War's turning points.

The Impact of Media on Public Perception

In the realm of historical events, few moments have had as significant an impact on public perception as the Bay of Pigs invasion and the Cuban Missile Crisis during the Cold War. These two critical turning points not only shaped the global balance of power but also revealed the role of media in influencing public opinion and ultimately, the decision-making of President John F. Kennedy.

Kennedy's Diluted Bay of Pigs Invasion Created One Year Later the Cuban Missile Crisis

One cannot discuss the impact of media on public perception without first acknowledging the diluted Bay of Pigs invasion and its subsequent effects. Kennedy's decision to proceed with a scaled-down military operation in Cuba was met with disastrous consequences, leading to the capture and humiliation of American-backed Cuban exiles. The media played a crucial role in exposing the failure of the invasion, resulting in a significant blow to Kennedy's credibility and reputation.

The Role of Cold War Politics in Shaping Kennedy's Decision-Making

Cold War politics played a crucial role in shaping Kennedy's decision-making during both the Bay of Pigs invasion and the Cuban Missile Crisis. The fear of Soviet expansion and the desire to maintain American credibility in the face of communism heavily influenced Kennedy's choices. It was this context that set the stage for the media's role in shaping public opinion and perception.

The Public Perception of Kennedy's Handling of the Bay of Pigs Invasion and the Cuban Missile Crisis

The media's portrayal of Kennedy's handling of these events significantly impacted public perception. The failure of the Bay of Pigs invasion cast doubt on Kennedy's ability to effectively navigate the Cold War landscape. However, his handling of the Cuban Missile Crisis, widely regarded as a success, restored public confidence in his leadership. The media's coverage of both events played a crucial role in shaping the public's perception of Kennedy's capabilities as a leader.

The Role of the Media in Shaping Public Opinion

During the Bay of Pigs invasion and the Cuban Missile Crisis, the media played a pivotal role in shaping public opinion. Through various mediums such as newspapers, television, and radio, journalists provided the public with information, images, and narratives that influenced their perception of the events unfolding. The media's ability to disseminate information quickly and widely altered public sentiment and ultimately impacted the decisions made by Kennedy and his administration.

The Significance of the Bay of Pigs Invasion and the Cuban Missile Crisis in Shaping the Global Balance of Power

Lastly, the Bay of Pigs invasion and the Cuban Missile Crisis had far-reaching consequences in shaping the global balance of power during the Cold War. These events heightened tensions between the United States and the Soviet Union, pushing both sides closer to the brink of nuclear war. The media's coverage of these events not only shaped public perception but also influenced the actions and reactions of world leaders, ultimately shaping the course of the Cold War itself.

In conclusion, the impact of media on public perception during the Bay of Pigs invasion and the Cuban Missile Crisis cannot be underestimated. The media's ability to shape public opinion influenced Kennedy's decision-making and had significant implications for the global balance of power during the Cold War. Understanding the role of media in historical events is crucial for historians seeking to analyze and interpret these pivotal moments in history.

The Media's Coverage of the Cuban Missile Crisis

The Cuban Missile Crisis is widely regarded as one of the most critical turning points of the Cold War. President John F. Kennedy's decisions during this crisis had far-reaching implications for the global balance of power. However, the role of the media in shaping public opinion and influencing Kennedy's decision-making cannot be understated.

The media played a significant role in shaping public perception during both the Bay of Pigs invasion and the Cuban Missile Crisis. The coverage of these events by the media was instrumental in creating a sense of urgency and fear among the American public. The media portrayed the events as a direct threat to national security, amplifying the tension and anxiety already present during the Cold War.

Kennedy's handling of the Bay of Pigs invasion was heavily criticized by the media. The failed invasion, which was intended to overthrow Fidel Castro's regime, was seen as a major setback for the United States. The media highlighted Kennedy's perceived indecisiveness and lack of support for the Cuban exiles, leading to a negative public perception of his leadership.

The media's coverage of the Cuban Missile Crisis was crucial in shaping public opinion and support for Kennedy's decisions. The media portrayed the crisis as a direct confrontation between the United States and the Soviet Union, emphasizing the potential for nuclear war. This coverage heightened public awareness and concern, putting pressure on Kennedy to take decisive action.

The media's role in shaping public opinion during the Cuban Missile Crisis also had an impact on Kennedy's decision-making. The intense media scrutiny and public pressure forced Kennedy to carefully consider the potential consequences of his actions. The media's portrayal of the crisis as a high-stakes game of brinkmanship influenced Kennedy's approach, leading him to pursue a diplomatic solution rather than a military one.

The significance of the Bay of Pigs invasion and the Cuban Missile Crisis cannot be overstated in shaping the global balance of power during the Cold War. The events highlighted the dangers of nuclear weapons and the need for effective diplomacy in resolving international conflicts. The media's coverage of these events played a crucial role in shaping public opinion and influencing Kennedy's decision-making, ultimately leading to a peaceful resolution of the crisis.

In conclusion, the media's coverage of the Cuban Missile Crisis had a profound impact on public perception, Kennedy's decision-making, and the global balance of power during the Cold War. The media's portrayal of the crisis as a direct threat to national security intensified public concern and pressured Kennedy to pursue a diplomatic solution. The significance of these events in shaping history cannot be understated, making the media's role in covering them a vital aspect of understanding this critical turning point of the Cold War.

The Tension and Dramatic Nature of the Crisis

The Cold War was a period of intense geopolitical rivalry and ideological conflict between the United States and the Soviet Union. Within this broader context, two pivotal moments stand out as turning points: the Bay of Pigs invasion and the Cuban Missile Crisis. These events were not only significant in their own right but also intimately connected, with the former directly leading to the latter. This subchapter explores the tension and dramatic nature of these crises, shedding light on their historical importance and impact.

Kennedy's diluted Bay of Pigs invasion in 1961 set the stage for the Cuban Missile Crisis that erupted just a year later. The failed invasion was an embarrassing setback for the United States, exposing the weaknesses in its intelligence and military planning. It also revealed Kennedy's cautious approach to foreign policy and his desire to avoid direct military confrontation with the Soviet Union. However, this diluted response inadvertently sent a signal of weakness to both the Soviets and the Cuban regime, leading them to believe that the United States could be pushed further.

The role of Cold War politics cannot be understated in shaping Kennedy's decision-making during these crises. The fear of communist expansion in the Western Hemisphere, coupled with the aggressive Soviet actions in Cuba, forced Kennedy into a corner. He had to balance the desire to protect American interests and contain communism with the need to avoid an all-out nuclear war. This delicate balancing act created immense tension and uncertainty, with the world holding its breath to see how events would unfold.

Public perception of Kennedy's handling of the Bay of Pigs invasion and the Cuban Missile Crisis was a crucial factor in shaping the political landscape at the time. The Bay of Pigs invasion was widely seen as a failure and damaged Kennedy's reputation. However, his handling of the Cuban Missile Crisis was perceived as a success, with the public praising his resolve and leadership. These perceptions had a profound impact on Kennedy's presidency and his ability to navigate the treacherous waters of the Cold War.

The media played a significant role in shaping public opinion during these crises. The intense media coverage brought the reality of the Cold War and the potential for nuclear conflict into people's living rooms. The vivid images and reports of the crisis heightened the tension and created a sense of urgency among the public. The media's ability to shape public opinion and influence policy decisions became evident during this period, highlighting the power of the fourth estate in a time of crisis.

Finally, the significance of the Bay of Pigs invasion and the Cuban Missile Crisis in shaping the global balance of power during the Cold War cannot be overstated. These events marked a turning point in the Cold War, with the United States and the Soviet Union coming perilously close to a nuclear confrontation. The crisis highlighted the dangers of brinkmanship and the need for diplomatic solutions to global conflicts. It also led to a reevaluation of nuclear weapons and the establishment of communication channels between the superpowers to prevent future crises.

In conclusion, the tension and dramatic nature of the Bay of Pigs invasion and the Cuban Missile Crisis were defining moments in the Cold War. These crises showcased the complexities of Cold War politics, the role of public opinion and the media, and the lasting impact on global power dynamics. Understanding these events is crucial for historians seeking to unravel the intricacies of this tumultuous period in world history.

The Role of Press Conferences and Presidential Addresses

During the Cold War, two crucial events occurred that shaped the global balance of power and heavily influenced President John F. Kennedy's decision-making: the Bay of Pigs invasion and the Cuban Missile Crisis. These events not only tested Kennedy's leadership skills but also had a profound impact on the public perception of his handling of these crises. The role of press conferences and presidential addresses cannot be underestimated in understanding the significance of these turning points in history.

Kennedy's diluted Bay of Pigs invasion, which took place in April 1961, was a failed attempt to overthrow Fidel Castro's communist regime in Cuba. One year later, this failure had unintended consequences, as it ultimately led to the Cuban Missile Crisis. Kennedy's decision-making during these events was heavily influenced by the Cold War politics of the time. The fear of Soviet expansion and the desire to maintain the United States' position as a global superpower played a significant role in shaping his responses.

The public perception of Kennedy's handling of the Bay of Pigs invasion and the Cuban Missile Crisis was a crucial factor in understanding the impact of these events. Press conferences and presidential addresses provided Kennedy with a platform to communicate his decisions and actions to the American people. These media interactions not only shaped public opinion but also influenced the global perception of the United States' response to these crises. Kennedy's ability to effectively address the nation during these times of uncertainty played a key role in maintaining public support and confidence in his leadership.

The media played a vital role in shaping public opinion during the Bay of Pigs invasion and the Cuban Missile Crisis. Journalists had unprecedented access to information and events, and their reporting had a profound impact on the public's understanding of the situation. The media's ability to shape public opinion and influence the course of events cannot be underestimated in understanding the significance of these crises.

Ultimately, the Bay of Pigs invasion and the Cuban Missile Crisis had far-reaching consequences in shaping the global balance of power during the Cold War. These events highlighted the dangers of nuclear brinkmanship and the importance of effective leadership in times of crisis. The role of press conferences and presidential addresses in shaping public opinion and influencing the course of events cannot be overlooked. Understanding the significance of these events requires a comprehensive analysis of the media's role, Kennedy's decision-making, and the public's perception of these crises. These turning points in history continue to be studied by historians to gain insight into the complexities of Cold War politics and the role of leadership in shaping the course of history.

Media Interpretation and Analysis of Kennedy's Actions

Throughout the Cold War, President John F. Kennedy faced numerous challenges that tested his leadership and decision-making abilities. Two of the most critical moments in his presidency were the Bay of Pigs invasion and the Cuban Missile Crisis. These events not only shaped Kennedy's legacy but also had a profound impact on the global balance of power during the Cold War.

Kennedy's Diluted Bay of Pigs Invasion Created One Year Later the Cuban Missile Crisis

The failed Bay of Pigs invasion in April 1961 demonstrated a significant turning point in Kennedy's foreign policy approach. The invasion, originally planned by the Central Intelligence Agency (CIA) during the Eisenhower administration, was aimed at overthrowing Fidel Castro's communist regime in Cuba. However, due to a series of miscommunications and poor execution, the invasion ended in disaster.

The role of Cold War politics in shaping Kennedy's decision-making during the Bay of Pigs invasion and the Cuban Missile Crisis

Cold War politics played a crucial role in shaping Kennedy's decision-making during these events. The United States was locked in a fierce rivalry with the Soviet Union, and Cuba had become a strategic outpost for the Soviets in the Western Hemisphere. Kennedy's actions were influenced by the fear of communist expansion and the desire to protect American national security interests.

The public perception of Kennedy's handling of the Bay of Pigs invasion and the Cuban Missile Crisis

The media played a vital role in shaping public opinion regarding Kennedy's handling of these crises. Initially, the media portrayed Kennedy as indecisive and weak after the Bay of Pigs failure. However, during the Cuban Missile Crisis, the media presented a more positive image of Kennedy as a strong and decisive leader. This shift in public perception can be attributed to Kennedy's handling of the crisis, which showcased his ability to navigate a dangerous and potentially catastrophic situation.

The role of the media in shaping public opinion during the Bay of Pigs invasion and the Cuban Missile Crisis

The media's coverage of the Bay of Pigs invasion and the Cuban Missile Crisis had a significant impact on public opinion. Journalists played a crucial role in shaping the narrative surrounding these events, influencing how the public perceived Kennedy's actions. The media's portrayal of Kennedy as a strong leader during the Cuban Missile Crisis helped bolster public support for his handling of the situation.

The significance of the Bay of Pigs invasion and the Cuban Missile Crisis in shaping the global balance of power during the Cold War

The Bay of Pigs invasion and the Cuban Missile Crisis had far-reaching implications for the global balance of power during the Cold War. The failure of the Bay of Pigs invasion demonstrated the limitations of American military power and emboldened the Soviet Union. The Cuban Missile Crisis brought the world to the brink of nuclear war but ultimately resulted in a diplomatic resolution that showcased Kennedy's ability to navigate the complexities of international relations.

In conclusion, the media's interpretation and analysis of Kennedy's actions during the Bay of Pigs invasion and the Cuban Missile Crisis played a significant role in shaping public opinion and the global balance of power during the Cold War. These events highlighted the challenges and complexities of leadership in a time of intense geopolitical tensions, and their impact on Kennedy's legacy cannot be understated. Historians continue to study and analyze these turning points to gain a deeper understanding of the Cold War era and its enduring significance.

The Legacy of Media Coverage

The legacy of media coverage surrounding the Bay of Pigs invasion and the Cuban Missile Crisis holds immense significance in understanding the pivotal events that shaped the global balance of power during the Cold War. This subchapter delves into the profound impact of media coverage on the public perception of Kennedy's decisions, the role of

Cold War politics in shaping his decision-making, and the enduring influence of these events on historical narratives.

The diluted Bay of Pigs invasion, which took place in 1961, would prove to be a crucial turning point in the Cold War and set the stage for the Cuban Missile Crisis a year later. Historians have closely examined the links between these two events, emphasizing how the failed invasion influenced Kennedy's decision-making process during the Cuban Missile Crisis. By analyzing the political context of the time, historians can gain valuable insights into the pressures and constraints that shaped Kennedy's responses.

A critical aspect of the legacy of these events lies in the public perception of Kennedy's handling of both the Bay of Pigs invasion and the Cuban Missile Crisis. The media played a pivotal role in shaping this perception, as their coverage had a profound impact on public opinion. This subchapter explores the ways in which the media influenced and shaped the narrative surrounding these events, highlighting the power of media in shaping public opinion during times of crisis and conflict.

The role of the media in both events was multifaceted. They served as key sources of information, disseminating news about the developments and decisions made by Kennedy and his administration. Simultaneously, they were instrumental in shaping public opinion through their analysis, interpretation, and presentation of these events. Historians studying the legacy of media coverage can examine the media's influence on public sentiment, and how it affected Kennedy's decision-making process.

Lastly, this subchapter emphasizes the profound impact of the Bay of Pigs invasion and the Cuban Missile Crisis in shaping the global balance of power during the Cold War. Both events had far-reaching consequences, not only for the United States but also for the Soviet

Union and other nations involved. By understanding the historical significance of these events, historians can better comprehend the long-lasting effects they had on international relations, nuclear deterrence strategies, and the overall trajectory of the Cold War.

In conclusion, the legacy of media coverage surrounding the Bay of Pigs invasion and the Cuban Missile Crisis is a crucial aspect of understanding the historical significance of these events. Historians studying Kennedy's decisions, the role of Cold War politics, public perception, and the global balance of power in the Cold War era can gain valuable insights from analyzing the media's influence. By exploring this subchapter, historians can deepen their understanding of these turning points and their enduring impact on the course of history.

The Power of Visual Imagery and Television Broadcasting

Television broadcasting played a pivotal role in shaping the public perception of President John F. Kennedy's decision-making during two crucial events of the Cold War - the Bay of Pigs invasion and the Cuban Missile Crisis. This subchapter explores the power of visual imagery and how it influenced the global balance of power during this critical period.

Kennedy's Diluted Bay of Pigs Invasion Created One Year Later the Cuban Missile Crisis

One of the turning points of the Cold War was Kennedy's diluted Bay of Pigs invasion in April 1961. This failed operation not only exposed the weaknesses of American intelligence and military planning but also had significant long-term consequences. The invasion's failure allowed Fidel Castro to strengthen his grip on power and seek support from the Soviet Union. This paved the way for the Cuban Missile Crisis, which unfolded just over a year later.

The Role of Cold War Politics in Shaping Kennedy's Decision-Making

Kennedy's decision-making during both the Bay of Pigs invasion and the Cuban Missile Crisis was heavily influenced by the complex dynamics of Cold War politics. The fear of Soviet expansion and the desire to appear strong and resolute in the face of communist aggression played a crucial role in shaping his actions. Understanding this context is essential for historians to grasp the motivations behind Kennedy's choices during these events.

The Public Perception of Kennedy's Handling of the Bay of Pigs Invasion and the Cuban Missile Crisis

The public perception of Kennedy's handling of these crises was greatly influenced by the power of visual imagery. Television broadcasts brought the reality of these events into the living rooms of millions of Americans. The graphic images of the failed invasion and the tense moments of the missile crisis had a profound impact on public opinion, shaping their views of Kennedy's leadership and decision-making abilities.

The Role of the Media in Shaping Public Opinion

The media played a crucial role in shaping public opinion during these critical moments of the Cold War. Television broadcasts not only provided live coverage of the events but also presented different narratives and interpretations. The media's ability to shape public opinion was further enhanced by the emergence of photojournalism, which captured powerful images that resonated with viewers and influenced their perception of the events.

The Significance of the Bay of Pigs Invasion and the Cuban Missile Crisis in Shaping the Global Balance of Power

Both the Bay of Pigs invasion and the Cuban Missile Crisis had far-reaching implications for the global balance of power during the Cold War. These events heightened tensions between the United States and the Soviet Union, bringing the world to the brink of nuclear war. The successful resolution of the missile crisis through diplomacy showcased the importance of communication and negotiation in managing international conflicts, setting a precedent for future Cold War confrontations.

In conclusion, the power of visual imagery and television broadcasting cannot be overstated in shaping public opinion and influencing decision-making during the Bay of Pigs invasion and the Cuban Missile Crisis. Understanding the role of the media and the significance of these events is crucial for historians seeking to comprehend the complexities of the Cold War and its impact on global politics.

The Influence of Journalistic Narratives on Historical Memory

Historians have long recognized the pivotal role that the Bay of Pigs invasion and the Cuban Missile Crisis played in shaping the course of the Cold War. These two events, both closely intertwined and occurring within a span of just over a year, not only tested the mettle of President John F. Kennedy but also had far-reaching implications for the global balance of power.

One of the key aspects that historians have focused on is the influence of journalistic narratives on the historical memory of these events. The media played a significant role in shaping public opinion during this critical period, and their portrayal of Kennedy's decisions had a profound impact on how these events were perceived by the American public and the international community at large.

The public perception of Kennedy's handling of the Bay of Pigs invasion and the Cuban Missile Crisis was heavily influenced by media coverage. Initially, the invasion was presented as a resounding failure, casting doubt on Kennedy's ability to effectively manage Cold War politics. The media highlighted the lack of coordination, intelligence failures, and political miscalculations that characterized the Bay of Pigs operation.

However, the narrative shifted dramatically during the Cuban Missile Crisis. The media portrayed Kennedy as a strong and decisive leader who successfully navigated the treacherous waters of Cold War politics. Journalistic narratives emphasized his resolve in the face of Soviet aggression and the ultimate resolution of the crisis through diplomatic means, thus averting a potentially catastrophic nuclear war.

These narratives not only shaped public opinion but also influenced historical memory. The perception of Kennedy's handling of these events has remained largely consistent with the media's portrayal at the time. This has had a lasting impact on how these events are remembered and interpreted by historians.

Furthermore, the significance of the Bay of Pigs invasion and the Cuban Missile Crisis in shaping the global balance of power during the Cold War cannot be understated. These events highlighted the escalating tensions between the United States and the Soviet Union, and the potential for nuclear confrontation. The media's coverage of these events played a crucial role in disseminating this information to the public and reinforcing the gravity of the situation.

In conclusion, the influence of journalistic narratives on historical memory is a crucial aspect to consider when examining the Bay of Pigs invasion and the Cuban Missile Crisis. The media's portrayal of Kennedy's decisions and their impact on public opinion have had a lasting impact on how these events are remembered today. Additionally, the significance of these events in shaping the global balance of power during the Cold War cannot be overlooked. It is essential for historians to critically analyze the media's role in shaping historical memory and to consider the broader implications of these narratives on our understanding of these crucial turning points in history.

The Media's Role in Shaping Public Opinion and Political Discourse

Throughout history, the media has played a crucial role in shaping public opinion and political discourse. This subchapter will delve into the specific ways in which the media influenced the public's perception of President John F. Kennedy's decisions during the Bay of Pigs invasion and the Cuban Missile Crisis, two pivotal events in the context of the Cold War.

One of the key aspects to explore is how Cold War politics influenced Kennedy's decision-making process during these events. By examining the global balance of power during the Cold War, historians can gain a deeper understanding of the pressures and considerations that shaped Kennedy's actions. This analysis will shed light on the complex and delicate nature of the decisions he had to make, as well as the consequences they had on the global stage.

Furthermore, it is crucial to explore the public perception of Kennedy's handling of these crises. The media played a significant role in shaping public opinion, often framing the events in a way that influenced how people viewed the president's actions. Understanding the nuances of public perception is essential in comprehending the impact it had on Kennedy's decision-making process and subsequent policies.

The media's influence on public opinion cannot be underestimated, particularly during times of crisis. Therefore, it is imperative to examine the role of the media in shaping public opinion during the Bay of Pigs invasion and the Cuban Missile Crisis. By analyzing the way news outlets reported on these events and the narratives they constructed, historians can gain insights into how media coverage impacted public sentiment and political discourse.

Lastly, this subchapter will highlight the significance of the Bay of Pigs invasion and the Cuban Missile Crisis in shaping the global balance of power during the Cold War. These events not only had immediate consequences but also had a lasting impact on the dynamics between the United States, the Soviet Union, and other global powers. By exploring this significance, historians can better understand the broader implications of these crises and their role in shaping the Cold War.

Overall, this subchapter will provide historians with a comprehensive analysis of the media's role in shaping public opinion and political discourse during the Bay of Pigs invasion and the Cuban Missile Crisis. By examining the interplay between media coverage, public perception, and Kennedy's decision-making process, a clearer understanding of these turning points in the Cold War can be achieved.

Chapter 5: The Significance of the Bay of Pigs Invasion and the Cuban Missile Crisis in Shaping the Global Balance of Power during the Cold War

The Impact on US-Soviet Relations

The period of the Cold War was characterized by intense rivalry and tensions between the United States and the Soviet Union. The decisions made by President John F. Kennedy during the Bay of Pigs invasion and the Cuban Missile Crisis had a profound impact on the course of US-Soviet relations, shaping the global balance of power during this critical era.

Kennedy's Diluted Bay of Pigs Invasion Created One Year Later the Cuban Missile Crisis:

One of the major turning points in the Cold War was Kennedy's decision to support the Bay of Pigs invasion in 1961. The failed attempt to overthrow Fidel Castro's regime in Cuba not only damaged US credibility but also led to a bitter setback in relations with the Soviet Union. The Soviets saw an opportunity to strengthen their alliance with Cuba and eventually led to the Cuban Missile Crisis in 1962.

The Role of Cold War Politics in Shaping Kennedy's Decision-making:

Kennedy's decision-making during the Bay of Pigs invasion and the Cuban Missile Crisis was heavily influenced by the dynamics of the Cold War. The fear of the spread of communism and the need to contain Soviet influence played a significant role in shaping his approach. Kennedy's commitment to the principle of containment and the belief that the United States had to take a tough stance against the Soviet Union were critical factors in his decision-making process.

The Public Perception of Kennedy's Handling of the Bay of Pigs Invasion and the Cuban Missile Crisis:

The way Kennedy handled these two crises had a significant impact on public perception. While the Bay of Pigs invasion was perceived as a failure, the successful resolution of the Cuban Missile Crisis was seen as a major victory for the United States. This perception of Kennedy as a strong leader who stood up against Soviet aggression helped boost his popularity and strengthen public support for his administration.

The Role of the Media in Shaping Public Opinion:

The media played a crucial role in shaping public opinion during the Bay of Pigs invasion and the Cuban Missile Crisis. The coverage of these events by the media greatly influenced public perception and the understanding of the stakes involved. The media's portrayal of Kennedy as a decisive and resolute leader during the Cuban Missile Crisis helped rally public support for his actions.

The Significance of the Bay of Pigs Invasion and the Cuban Missile Crisis in Shaping the Global Balance of Power:

The Bay of Pigs invasion and the Cuban Missile Crisis had far-reaching implications for the global balance of power during the Cold War. The United States' failure in the Bay of Pigs invasion highlighted the limits of its power and emboldened the Soviet Union. However, the successful resolution of the Cuban Missile Crisis allowed the United States to demonstrate its resolve and put the Soviet Union on notice. This event marked a crucial shift in the balance of power, as it showed that the United States would not tolerate the presence of Soviet missiles in its backyard.

In conclusion, the decisions made by Kennedy during the Bay of Pigs invasion and the Cuban Missile Crisis had a lasting impact on US-Soviet relations. These events shaped the global balance of power during the Cold War and influenced public perception of Kennedy's leadership. The role of cold war politics, the media, and public opinion cannot be understated in understanding the significance of these events. Historians must analyze these turning points to fully comprehend the complexities of this critical period in world history.

Escalation of Tensions and the Risk of Nuclear War

The Escalation of Tensions and the Risk of Nuclear War

Introduction:

The Cold War's Turning Points: Kennedy's Decisions in the Bay of Pigs and Cuban Missile Crisis delves into the critical moments that shaped the course of the Cold War. This subchapter titled "Escalation of Tensions and the Risk of Nuclear War" explores the dangerous path the world was on during the Bay of Pigs invasion and the Cuban Missile Crisis. Addressed to historians, this subchapter aims to provide a comprehensive analysis of the events and their significance in shaping the global balance of power during the Cold War.

Kennedy's Diluted Bay of Pigs Invasion Created One Year Later the Cuban Missile Crisis:

One of the key aspects discussed in this subchapter is the direct link between Kennedy's diluted Bay of Pigs invasion and the subsequent Cuban Missile Crisis. By examining Kennedy's decision-making during the Bay of Pigs invasion, historians gain insights into the factors that contributed to the escalation of tensions, ultimately leading to the risk of nuclear war.

The Role of Cold War Politics in Shaping Kennedy's Decision-Making:

The subchapter explores the intricate role of Cold War politics in influencing Kennedy's decision-making process during these critical events. By analyzing the global geopolitical landscape, historians gain a deeper understanding of the pressures and considerations that influenced Kennedy's actions.

Public Perception of Kennedy's Handling:

Furthermore, this subchapter delves into the public perception of Kennedy's handling of the Bay of Pigs invasion and the Cuban Missile Crisis. By examining public opinion at the time, historians can evaluate the impact of Kennedy's decisions on the nation and the world.

The Role of Media in Shaping Public Opinion:

The media played a crucial role in shaping public opinion during these events. This subchapter examines the media's influence on public perception, shedding light on the strategies employed by the government and the media themselves to control the narrative surrounding the Bay of Pigs invasion and the Cuban Missile Crisis.

Significance in Shaping the Global Balance of Power:

Finally, this subchapter explores the enduring significance of the Bay of Pigs invasion and the Cuban Missile Crisis in shaping the global balance of power during the Cold War. By analyzing the long-term consequences of these events, historians gain a comprehensive understanding of their impact on the Cold War dynamics.

Conclusion:

"Escalation of Tensions and the Risk of Nuclear War" provides historians with a detailed analysis of the Bay of Pigs invasion and the Cuban Missile Crisis. By exploring Kennedy's decision-making, public perception, media influence, and the global balance of power, this subchapter offers a comprehensive understanding of these critical turning points in the Cold War.

Negotiations and Diplomatic Efforts to Deescalate

During the height of the Cold War, President John F. Kennedy found himself facing two critical turning points that would shape the course of history – the Bay of Pigs invasion and the Cuban Missile Crisis. In the aftermath of these events, Kennedy's decisions were crucial in not only preventing nuclear war but also in redefining the dynamics of global power. This subchapter explores the negotiations and diplomatic efforts employed by Kennedy to deescalate tensions and navigate through these treacherous waters.

Kennedy's diluted Bay of Pigs invasion, launched in April 1961, marked a significant failure in U.S. covert operations. The invasion, aimed at overthrowing Fidel Castro's regime in Cuba, was ill-planned and poorly executed. Recognizing the need to avoid further military escalation, Kennedy quickly shifted his focus towards diplomatic solutions. He initiated back-channel negotiations with the Soviet Union, seeking to find a peaceful resolution and prevent further damage to U.S.-Soviet relations.

The Cuban Missile Crisis, which unfolded in October 1962, brought the world to the brink of nuclear war. Kennedy's handling of the crisis was a delicate balancing act, as he faced pressure from both his advisors advocating for military action and those pushing for diplomatic solutions. Understanding the potential catastrophic consequences of a military confrontation, Kennedy opted for negotiations and diplomatic efforts to deescalate the situation.

Kennedy engaged in secret negotiations with Soviet Premier Nikita Khrushchev, exchanging letters and exploring compromises. Through back-channel communications, Kennedy was able to convey his commitment to a peaceful resolution while also making it clear that the U.S. would not tolerate the presence of nuclear weapons in Cuba. This diplomatic approach, coupled with a naval blockade and a show of military force, ultimately led to a peaceful resolution. Khrushchev agreed to remove the missiles from Cuba, and the crisis was averted.

The negotiations and diplomatic efforts employed by Kennedy during these critical moments had far-reaching implications. They not only prevented a nuclear war but also reshaped the global balance of power during the Cold War. Kennedy's ability to navigate through these crises and find diplomatic solutions demonstrated the importance of strategic thinking and negotiation in international relations.

In conclusion, negotiations and diplomatic efforts played a pivotal role in deescalating the tensions surrounding the Bay of Pigs invasion and the Cuban Missile Crisis. Kennedy's decisions to pursue diplomatic solutions rather than military escalation showcased his leadership and ability to navigate through perilous times. These events served as turning points during the Cold War, highlighting the significance of negotiations and diplomacy in shaping the global balance of power.

The Long-Term Effects on Superpower Dynamics

The Cold War's Turning Points: Kennedy's Decisions in the Bay of Pigs and Cuban Missile Crisis

Introduction:

The events surrounding the Bay of Pigs invasion and the Cuban Missile Crisis were pivotal moments in the history of the Cold War. President John F. Kennedy's decision-making during these crises had far-reaching consequences that shaped the global balance of power for years to come. This subchapter will delve into the long-term effects on superpower dynamics resulting from Kennedy's actions during these critical moments.

Kennedy's Diluted Bay of Pigs Invasion Created One Year Later the Cuban Missile Crisis:

One of the long-term effects of the Bay of Pigs invasion was its direct link to the Cuban Missile Crisis. Kennedy's decision to proceed with a watered-down version of the invasion, which resulted in failure, led to a loss of credibility for the United States. This emboldened Soviet Premier Nikita Khrushchev to deploy nuclear missiles in Cuba, sparking the most dangerous standoff of the Cold War.

The Role of Cold War Politics in Shaping Kennedy's Decision-Making:

Cold War politics heavily influenced Kennedy's decision-making process during the Bay of Pigs invasion and the Cuban Missile Crisis. The fear of appearing weak in the face of communism and the pressure to maintain the perception of a superpower led Kennedy to make certain choices that ultimately escalated tensions between the United States and the Soviet Union.

The Public Perception of Kennedy's Handling of the Crises:

The way Kennedy handled the Bay of Pigs invasion and the Cuban Missile Crisis had a significant impact on public opinion. While the failure of the invasion initially damaged his reputation, Kennedy's resolute stance during the missile crisis restored public confidence in his leadership. This perception influenced future political decisions and shaped public sentiment regarding the Cold War.

The Role of the Media in Shaping Public Opinion:

The media played a crucial role in shaping public opinion during these crises. Their coverage of the events, including the failure of the Bay of Pigs invasion and the tense standoff during the Cuban Missile Crisis, influenced how the American people perceived Kennedy's leadership. The media's portrayal of the events also had ripple effects on international perceptions of the United States and the Soviet Union.

The Significance of the Crises in Shaping the Global Balance of Power:

The Bay of Pigs invasion and the Cuban Missile Crisis had profound implications for the global balance of power during the Cold War. These events highlighted the dangers of brinkmanship and the potential catastrophic consequences of nuclear conflict. The resolution of the Cuban Missile Crisis, with Kennedy's successful negotiation with Khrushchev, demonstrated the importance of diplomacy in preventing a nuclear war and reshaped the dynamics between the superpowers.

Conclusion:

Kennedy's decisions during the Bay of Pigs invasion and the Cuban Missile Crisis had long-term effects on superpower dynamics. These events not only shaped public perception and influenced future political decisions but also highlighted the importance of diplomacy in preventing nuclear conflict. The legacy of these crises continues to be studied and analyzed by historians, offering valuable insights into the complexities of the Cold War and its impact on global politics.

Global Repercussions and the Cold War Proxy Conflicts

The Cold War was a period of intense geopolitical tension between the United States and the Soviet Union, which had global repercussions that were felt in various proxy conflicts around the world. This subchapter delves into the impact of these conflicts and how they shaped the global balance of power during the Cold War era.

One of the key turning points in the Cold War was the Bay of Pigs invasion, which was a failed attempt by the United States to overthrow the Cuban government under Fidel Castro. This invasion, although unsuccessful, had significant repercussions. It not only damaged the reputation of President John F. Kennedy but also heightened tensions between the United States and the Soviet Union. The failed invasion created a power vacuum that the Soviet Union capitalized on by placing nuclear weapons in Cuba, leading to the Cuban Missile Crisis a year later.

Kennedy's decision-making during both the Bay of Pigs invasion and the Cuban Missile Crisis was heavily influenced by Cold War politics. The fear of Soviet expansionism and the desire to maintain American hegemony shaped Kennedy's actions and responses. The subchapter explores how the geopolitical context of the Cold War influenced Kennedy's approach to these crises and how he navigated the delicate balance between deterrence and avoiding nuclear war.

Public perception of Kennedy's handling of these crises played a crucial role in shaping the narrative surrounding these events. The subchapter delves into the public's understanding and reactions to the Bay of Pigs invasion and the Cuban Missile Crisis, examining how Kennedy's leadership was perceived and the impact it had on his presidency.

Furthermore, the media played a significant role in shaping public opinion during these crises. The subchapter analyzes the media coverage of both events, highlighting the role of the press in influencing public perception and the impact it had on the decision-making process.

Finally, the subchapter explores the significance of the Bay of Pigs invasion and the Cuban Missile Crisis in shaping the global balance of power during the Cold War. These events marked a turning point in the conflict, leading to a heightened arms race and increased tensions between the superpowers. The subchapter examines the long-term consequences of these events and their impact on the global geopolitical landscape.

In conclusion, "Global Repercussions and the Cold War Proxy Conflicts" delves into the historical significance of the Bay of Pigs invasion and the Cuban Missile Crisis. It examines Kennedy's decision-making, public perception, the role of the media, and the overall impact of these events on the global balance of power during the Cold War era.

The Spread of Revolutionary Movements and Support for Castro

During the height of the Cold War, the spread of revolutionary movements and the support for Fidel Castro's regime in Cuba played a crucial role in shaping the global balance of power. This subchapter explores the factors that contributed to the rise of revolutionary movements in Latin America and the widespread support for Castro's socialist government.

One year after Kennedy's diluted Bay of Pigs invasion, the world witnessed the Cuban Missile Crisis, a direct consequence of Cold War politics. The failed invasion had inadvertently strengthened Castro's position both domestically and internationally. The invasion's failure exposed the vulnerabilities of the United States and its inability to overthrow the Castro regime, leading to a surge in support for Castro among the Cuban population. This support further fueled the spread of revolutionary movements across Latin America, as Castro became a symbol of resistance against American imperialism.

Cold War politics heavily influenced Kennedy's decision-making during the Bay of Pigs invasion and the Cuban Missile Crisis. The fear of communist expansion, especially in the Western Hemisphere, played a significant role in shaping Kennedy's approach to these crises. The United States' perceived vulnerability to Soviet influence in its own backyard heightened the stakes for Kennedy, leading him to make decisions that were driven by the need to preserve American credibility and deter further Soviet aggression.

Public perception of Kennedy's handling of these crises was mixed. While some praised his resolve during the Cuban Missile Crisis, the

Bay of Pigs invasion was widely seen as a failure. Kennedy faced criticism for his initial approval of the invasion plan and subsequent reluctance to provide air support during the operation. However, his handling of the Cuban Missile Crisis, which successfully avoided a nuclear war, boosted his public image and solidified his reputation as a strong leader.

The media played a pivotal role in shaping public opinion during these crises. The coverage of the Bay of Pigs invasion and the Cuban Missile Crisis influenced how the public perceived Kennedy's handling of these events. The media's portrayal of Kennedy as a decisive leader during the Cuban Missile Crisis helped to bolster his image, while the negative coverage of the Bay of Pigs invasion contributed to public disillusionment with the administration's foreign policy.

Ultimately, the Bay of Pigs invasion and the Cuban Missile Crisis were turning points in the Cold War. These events demonstrated the limitations of American power and the resilience of revolutionary movements in the face of external aggression. The support for Castro and the spread of revolutionary ideologies in Latin America had a profound impact on the global balance of power, as it challenged American hegemony and contributed to the polarization of the Cold War world. Understanding the significance of these events is crucial for historians studying the dynamics of the Cold War and the role of the United States in shaping global politics during this era.

The Influence on Latin American Politics and US Interventions

Throughout the Cold War, Latin American politics became a crucial battleground for the United States and the Soviet Union, with the region serving as a key arena for ideological competition and power struggles. This subchapter examines the significant influence of Latin American politics on US interventions, focusing on the pivotal role played by President John F. Kennedy in two critical events: the Bay of Pigs invasion and the Cuban Missile Crisis.

Kennedy's Diluted Bay of Pigs Invasion Created One Year Later the Cuban Missile Crisis

The failed Bay of Pigs invasion in April 1961 had far-reaching consequences for both US-Latin American relations and the global balance of power. The invasion, intended to overthrow Fidel Castro's communist regime in Cuba, was poorly planned and executed, resulting in a humiliating defeat for the US. This defeat motivated Castro to seek protection from the Soviet Union, ultimately leading to the Cuban Missile Crisis in October 1962.

The Role of Cold War Politics in Shaping Kennedy's Decision-Making

Kennedy's decision-making during both the Bay of Pigs invasion and the Cuban Missile Crisis was heavily influenced by the broader context of the Cold War. The prevailing anti-communist sentiment in the US and the fear of Soviet expansionism drove Kennedy to take a strong stance against Castro's Cuba. However, the Bay of Pigs invasion revealed the limitations of US military power and the complexities of intervening in foreign affairs without international support.

The Public Perception of Kennedy's Handling

The public perception of Kennedy's handling of these events was mixed. The failure of the Bay of Pigs invasion initially damaged his credibility, leading to criticism from both the American public and the international community. However, Kennedy's handling of the Cuban Missile Crisis, particularly his deft negotiation with Soviet Premier Nikita Khrushchev, was widely praised, solidifying his image as a strong and capable leader.

The Role of Media in Shaping Public Opinion

During both the Bay of Pigs invasion and the Cuban Missile Crisis, the role of the media in shaping public opinion was significant. The media's coverage of the failed invasion exposed the shortcomings of the US government's decision-making and raised doubts about the effectiveness of its anti-communist policies. Conversely, the media's coverage of the Cuban Missile Crisis highlighted Kennedy's resolve and skillful diplomacy, contributing to a more positive public perception.

The Significance in Shaping the Global Balance of Power

The Bay of Pigs invasion and the Cuban Missile Crisis had profound implications for the global balance of power during the Cold War. The failed invasion fueled Soviet confidence in supporting communist regimes in Latin America and elsewhere, while the Cuban Missile Crisis brought the world to the brink of nuclear war. These events underscored the precariousness of the Cold War era and the need for diplomatic solutions to prevent catastrophic consequences.

In conclusion, the influence of Latin American politics on US interventions during the Cold War, particularly in the context of the Bay of Pigs invasion and the Cuban Missile Crisis, cannot be understated. Understanding the complexities of these events is crucial for historians seeking to comprehend the interplay between ideology, power, and the global dynamics of the era.

The Heightened Arms Race and Nuclear Deterrence

Throughout the Cold War, the arms race between the United States and the Soviet Union reached unprecedented levels of intensity. The events surrounding the Bay of Pigs invasion and the Cuban Missile Crisis served as turning points, further escalating this competition and heightening the importance of nuclear deterrence in global politics.

Kennedy's Diluted Bay of Pigs Invasion Created One Year Later the Cuban Missile Crisis

One year after the ill-fated Bay of Pigs invasion in April 1961, the world found itself on the brink of nuclear war during the Cuban Missile Crisis. The failed invasion, which aimed to overthrow Fidel Castro's regime, not only exposed the weaknesses in American intelligence and military planning but also provoked the Soviet Union to increase its support for Cuba. This direct threat to American security led to the deployment of Soviet missiles in Cuba, which triggered the most dangerous standoff of the Cold War.

The Role of Cold War Politics in Shaping Kennedy's Decision-Making

Kennedy's decision-making during both the Bay of Pigs invasion and the Cuban Missile Crisis was heavily influenced by the overarching context of the Cold War. The fear of communist expansion, the need to maintain American credibility, and the pressure to demonstrate strength in the face of Soviet aggression all played a significant role in shaping his actions. The global power struggle between the United States and the Soviet Union dictated the stakes and consequences of every decision made.

The Public Perception of Kennedy's Handling of the Crisis

The way Kennedy handled both the Bay of Pigs invasion and the Cuban Missile Crisis had a profound impact on public opinion. Initially, the failure of the Bay of Pigs invasion damaged Kennedy's image, as it was seen as a major blunder. However, his skillful handling of the Cuban Missile Crisis, which involved a careful balance between diplomatic negotiations and military pressure, restored public confidence in his leadership. The public saw Kennedy as a strong and decisive leader who successfully navigated the dangerous waters of the Cold War.

The Role of the Media in Shaping Public Opinion

The media played a crucial role in shaping public opinion during these critical moments of the Cold War. The intense coverage of the Bay of Pigs invasion and the Cuban Missile Crisis by both American and international media outlets influenced public perception of the events and Kennedy's handling of them. The media's reporting and analysis framed the narrative, creating an atmosphere of tension and anxiety among the general public, while also scrutinizing the decisions made by the Kennedy administration.

The Significance of the Bay of Pigs Invasion and the Cuban Missile Crisis in Shaping the Global Balance of Power

Both the Bay of Pigs invasion and the Cuban Missile Crisis had a profound impact on the global balance of power during the Cold War. The events served as a wake-up call for the United States, highlighting the need for a more robust and effective strategy to counter Soviet influence. The Cuban Missile Crisis, in particular, led to a period of détente and increased emphasis on nuclear deterrence, as both superpowers recognized the dangers of direct confrontation. The heightened arms race that ensued shaped global politics for years to come, with nuclear weapons becoming the ultimate deterrent in international relations.

In conclusion, the heightened arms race and nuclear deterrence were central themes in the Cold War, and the Bay of Pigs invasion and the Cuban Missile Crisis served as critical turning points in this competition. The events surrounding these two incidents not only shaped Kennedy's decision-making but also had lasting effects on public perception, media influence, and the global balance of power. Understanding these dynamics is crucial for historians studying this pivotal era in world history.

Lessons Learned and Policy Shifts

The Cold War's Turning Points: Kennedy's Decisions in the Bay of Pigs and Cuban Missile Crisis

In the annals of history, few moments have had as profound an impact on the course of the Cold War as the Bay of Pigs invasion and the Cuban Missile Crisis. These two events, both occurring during President John F. Kennedy's administration, marked critical turning points that reshaped global politics and forever altered the balance of power between the United States and the Soviet Union. For historians, understanding the lessons learned and policy shifts that emerged from these crises is crucial to comprehending the broader narrative of the Cold War.

One of the most significant lessons learned from Kennedy's diluted Bay of Pigs invasion was the importance of accurate intelligence and thorough planning. The failed operation to overthrow Fidel Castro's regime in Cuba exposed the flaws in the CIA's intelligence gathering and the lack of coordination between various agencies. This realization led to a reassessment of intelligence methods and a renewed emphasis on careful planning and thorough analysis in future military endeavors.

Another crucial lesson was the role of Cold War politics in shaping Kennedy's decision-making during these crises. The fear of Communist expansion and the ideological battle between capitalism and communism played a central role in driving Kennedy's actions. The Bay of Pigs invasion and the discovery of Soviet missiles in Cuba were seen as direct threats to American security and reinforced the notion that the United States had to take decisive action to protect its interests.

Public perception of Kennedy's handling of these crises was also a significant aspect that shaped policy shifts. The Bay of Pigs invasion was widely viewed as a failure, leading to a decline in public confidence in the administration's ability to handle foreign policy matters. However, Kennedy's firm stance during the Cuban Missile Crisis, coupled with his skillful communication with the American people, restored public trust and bolstered his reputation as a strong leader.

The role of the media cannot be underestimated in shaping public opinion during these events. The press played a crucial role in exposing the shortcomings of the Bay of Pigs invasion and highlighting the gravity of the Cuban Missile Crisis. This increased scrutiny forced the Kennedy administration to be more transparent in its decision-making processes and ultimately influenced policy shifts in favor of more cautious and diplomatic approaches.

Finally, the Bay of Pigs invasion and the Cuban Missile Crisis had a profound impact on the global balance of power during the Cold War. The events demonstrated the vulnerability of the United States and the Soviet Union, leading both superpowers to recognize the dangers of direct confrontation. This realization paved the way for more nuanced and strategic approaches to managing the Cold War, such as the establishment of a hotline between Washington and Moscow to prevent future misunderstandings.

In conclusion, the Bay of Pigs invasion and the Cuban Missile Crisis were pivotal moments in the Cold War. The lessons learned and policy shifts that emerged from these events had far-reaching consequences, influencing intelligence gathering, decision-making processes, public perception, media involvement, and the global balance of power. Historians must study these turning points to grasp the complexities of the Cold War and the lasting impact of Kennedy's decisions.

Reevaluating Covert Operations and Interventionism

The Bay of Pigs invasion and the Cuban Missile Crisis are two of the most significant events in the history of the Cold War. These events not only shaped the global balance of power during this time but also had a profound impact on the decision-making process of President John

F. Kennedy. In this subchapter, we will delve into the various aspects surrounding these events, including their relationship, Kennedy's handling of them, and the role of public perception and the media in shaping the outcome.

One of the key arguments put forth in this subchapter is that Kennedy's diluted Bay of Pigs invasion created the conditions that led to the Cuban Missile Crisis one year later. The failed invasion in 1961, which aimed to overthrow Fidel Castro's regime, not only exposed the United States' covert operations but also led to increased Soviet involvement in Cuba. This ultimately resulted in the installation of nuclear missiles on the island, triggering the Cuban Missile Crisis in 1962.

Furthermore, this subchapter explores the role of Cold War politics in shaping Kennedy's decision-making during these events. The Cold War context, characterized by intense geopolitical rivalry between the United States and the Soviet Union, influenced Kennedy's actions and the strategies employed. It was this backdrop that led to the initiation of covert operations and interventionism in the first place.

The public perception of Kennedy's handling of both the Bay of Pigs invasion and the Cuban Missile Crisis is another crucial aspect examined in this subchapter. Kennedy's initial failure at the Bay of Pigs invasion garnered widespread criticism, casting doubts on his ability to effectively handle the growing tensions between the United States and the Soviet Union. However, his handling of the Cuban Missile Crisis was widely praised, showcasing his leadership skills and the importance of crisis management in the face of potential nuclear conflict.

Additionally, the role of media in shaping public opinion during these events is explored. The media played a significant role in disseminating information, influencing public perception, and shaping national and international narratives surrounding these events. The subchapter delves into the media's portrayal of Kennedy's decisions and actions, and the subsequent impact on public sentiment.

Finally, this subchapter highlights the significance of the Bay of Pigs invasion and the Cuban Missile Crisis in shaping the global balance of power during the Cold War. These events heightened tensions between the United States and the Soviet Union and illustrated the potential catastrophic consequences of the nuclear arms race. The subchapter explores how these events altered the dynamics of the Cold War and the subsequent arms control negotiations that followed.

In conclusion, the Bay of Pigs invasion and the Cuban Missile Crisis were pivotal moments in the Cold War. This subchapter provides a comprehensive analysis of these events, examining their relationship, Kennedy's decision-making, public perception, media influence, and the global impact. By reevaluating covert operations and interventionism, historians gain a deeper understanding of the complexities and consequences of these events, thus shedding light on the broader Cold War narrative.

The Focus on Diplomatic Engagement and Negotiations

During the height of the Cold War, President John F. Kennedy faced two critical moments that would forever shape his presidency and the global balance of power: the Bay of Pigs invasion and the Cuban Missile Crisis. These events not only tested Kennedy's leadership skills but also highlighted the importance of diplomatic engagement and negotiations in resolving international conflicts.

Kennedy's Diluted Bay of Pigs Invasion Created One Year Later the Cuban Missile Crisis

The Bay of Pigs invasion, launched in April 1961, was a covert operation aimed at overthrowing Fidel Castro's communist government in Cuba. However, due to a series of missteps and miscalculations, the invasion was poorly executed and ended in disaster. This failed attempt to remove Castro from power not only weakened the United States' credibility but also pushed Castro closer to the Soviet Union. It was this proximity to the Soviet Union that ultimately led to the Cuban Missile Crisis in October 1962. The lessons learned from the Bay of Pigs invasion highlighted the need for a more diplomatic approach in dealing with Castro's regime.

The Role of Cold War Politics in Shaping Kennedy's Decision-Making

Kennedy's decision-making during the Bay of Pigs invasion and the Cuban Missile Crisis was heavily influenced by the political climate of the Cold War. The fear of communism spreading throughout the Western Hemisphere, coupled with the ongoing arms race between the United States and the Soviet Union, put immense pressure on Kennedy to take decisive action. However, Kennedy recognized the importance of diplomacy in resolving these crises and sought peaceful solutions through negotiations.

The Public Perception of Kennedy's Handling of the Crises

The way Kennedy handled the Bay of Pigs invasion and the Cuban Missile Crisis was subject to intense scrutiny and shaped public perception of his leadership. Initially, the Bay of Pigs invasion was seen as a failure, leading to a decline in public support for Kennedy. However, his handling of the Cuban Missile Crisis, wherein he successfully negotiated the removal of Soviet missiles from Cuba, restored his reputation as a strong and capable leader. This public perception further emphasized the significance of diplomatic engagement in resolving conflicts and maintaining global stability.

The Role of Media in Shaping Public Opinion

The media played a crucial role in shaping public opinion during the Bay of Pigs invasion and the Cuban Missile Crisis. The coverage of these events highlighted the importance of accurate and timely information dissemination to the public. The media's role in providing updates and analysis of the crises also underscored the need for transparency and open communication in international affairs. Kennedy recognized the power of the media and employed strategic messaging to help shape public opinion and maintain support for his diplomatic efforts.

The Significance of the Crises in Shaping the Global Balance of Power

Both the Bay of Pigs invasion and the Cuban Missile Crisis had far-reaching implications for the global balance of power during the Cold War. The failed invasion highlighted the limitations of military interventions and the need for diplomatic solutions. The Cuban Missile Crisis, on the other hand, showcased the effectiveness of negotiations in resolving conflicts and preventing a nuclear war between the superpowers. These events served as turning points in the Cold War, leading to a shift in global dynamics and a greater emphasis on diplomatic engagement and negotiations as a means to achieve peace and stability.

In conclusion, the Bay of Pigs invasion and the Cuban Missile Crisis were pivotal moments in history that highlighted the significance of diplomatic engagement and negotiations. Kennedy's decisions during these crises were shaped by the political climate of the Cold War and the public perception of his leadership. The media played a critical role in shaping public opinion, emphasizing the importance of accurate information dissemination. Ultimately, these events reshaped the global balance of power during the Cold War, emphasizing the need for diplomatic solutions to international conflicts.